To The
Edmond J. Safra Synagogue

With Best Wishes

703 AMERICAN SEPHARDIM

DIVERSITY WITHIN COHESIVENESS

703 AMERICAN SEPHARDIM

DIVERSITY WITHIN COHESIVENESS

DR. JUDITH MIZRAHI

Gemini
Books

205 East 69th Street
New York, NY 10021

Based on the Dissertation submitted to
New York University, 1987:

Mizrahi, Judith. (1987) <u>Sources of diversity</u>
<u>in Sephardim</u>. UMI # 8720134. Ann Arbor, MI:
University Microfilms, Inc.

ISBN: 0-9635425-0-8

Published by Gemini Books
205 East 69th Street
New York, New York 10021

To my mother --
who appreciated me and showed it.
She was rare, so complete.
A woman of beauty, kindness and backbone,
style, balance and integrity, humor, vitality and courage.
A joy has passed. Our love remains.
She sees me through life.
This book is for and because of
Rose Musikantow Mizrahi.

9/22/15 - 6/4/93

"It is not so much what you say in a book that constitutes its value . . . (but) all you would like to say, which nourishes it secretly."

--Andre Gide

CONTENTS

Tables

Illustrations

Endorsements

A leader in the Sephardic community and the three sponsors from New York University of the author's dissertation have indicated their support of the preparation of this monograph. The Haham, Rabbi Solomon Gaon, Professor Stein and Professor Merrifield have addressed their comments to the reader; Professor Hamburger, the chairperson of the sponsoring committee, has addressed his to the author. The author is grateful for their continuing encouragement.

From The Haham, Rabbi Solomon Gaon

Dr. Judith Mizrahi has done what I would call "pioneering work." Her study is a major contribution. It is rigorously controlled research, done with a great deal of thought, care, reading and careful and original analyses. Her work is important not only because it is educative as it stands but also because it provides a sound basis for future research on the Sephardim of the United States. I applaud the final product.

> The Haham, Rabbi Solomon Gaon, Ph.D.
> Chief Rabbi of the World Sephardi
>   Federation
> President of the Union of the Sephardic
>   Congregations of America and Canada
> Holder of the Chair of Sephardic Studies
>   at Yeshiva University
> Holder of the Maybaum Chair in the
>   Rabbinics at Yeshiva University

From Professor Hamburger:

Dear Judith,

I have read the summary of your research which is now available to a much larger audience than usually is reached by the dissertation channels. As familiar as I am with your study, reading the report in this form confirmed for me again what an excellent and meaningful research it is. It is not only serious, rigorous and scholarly but it is also that miracle of miracles--interesting reading.

For one thing, the background and rationale for the research stand on their own as fascinating and important. Your devotion to exploring in depth what some might consider a footnote to American Jewish history is thoroughly justified insofar as the depths of meaning involved in the Sephardic experience are revealed. Thus, what emerges is both significant insight into a particularly interesting historical and social phenomenon as well as a contribution to psychological research methods. It is clear that you have mastered state of the art scale technique, complex theory of ethnic identity, and American Jewish sociology, but what is equally clear is that you have successfully synthesized all this into a useful, informative and interesting report suitable to the general reader.

I am therefore very pleased to see this culmination of your study made available to a wider readership. My warmest congratulations to you.

Sincerely,

Martin Hamburger, Ph.D.
Professor Emeritus, New York
 University,
Distinguished Adjunct Professor,
 Florida International University

From Professor Stein:

In a world constantly in flux how does a person stay sane? No answer to this question is more crucial than Ethnic Identity.

Ethnic Identity, rooted in the past, is psychologically functional in the present. It provides emotional succor when we become socially marginal, isolated, or rejected so that we never suffer the debilitating effects of ever feeling really alone. Knowledge of our people's history, the difficulties they endured and the problems they solved prepare us for the complexities in our daily lives and facilitate our efforts to contribute creatively to the future.

The significance of Ethnic Identity is not limited to the individual. It also makes significant contributions at the societal and cultural levels. Sharing of ethnic histories and traditions enriches the lives of all. Cultures grow and develop from the transactional relationships between different ethnic groups. Civilizations evolve from a complex process of accepting and integrating ethnic differences. The homogenization of groups leads to the loss of social vitality and to cultural decay.

For all of the above reasons, the work undertaken by Dr. Mizrahi is most important. But, they have always been important. What is unique in Dr. Mizrahi's contribution is that she provides us with a rigorous and valid methodology to test hypotheses derived from assertions just presented. Her work therefore is a milestone in the study of Ethnic Identity. Her contributions to date augur well for her creative efforts in the future. They will enrich all our lives. Hers will be an exciting career to follow.

Morris I. Stein, Ph.D.
Professor of Psychology
New York University

From Professor Merrifield:

From time to time, a professor has the good fortune to be asked to serve a student in an effort that is truly unfamiliar in many ways. These situations make us grow, and often provide us with much more than we give. So it has been with Dr. Judith Mizrahi and her dissertation on diversity and communality among Sephardim.

I had been aware of the Jewish contributions to philosophy and religious thought, but I did not realize the degree to which the Jewish people had diversified as they adapted to their varied environments throughout history; even the major distinction between Sephardim and Ashkenazim was new to me. When the subdivisions of Sephardim were discussed, and later supported by survey evidence, I was at once amazed by the result and gratified that the utility of the data analytic methods I had suggested was so evident.

Dr. Mizrahi demonstrated what her intuition had told her is true--that Sephardim can be differentiated in terms of national groups, all the while maintaining a communality of liturgy and custom that provides a strong anchor for their identity as Sephardim. Her persistence in this work was remarkable. On occasion, she came to me almost ready to discontinue it; fortunately, as we talked, she realized anew that her commitment to herself and to those with whom she shares the Sephardic heritage could not be set aside. She learned much from her months of study in the library and her assiduous pursuit of the experts whose judgments of Sephardic characteristics are so central to the final result. Working with her through the seemingly endless cycle of analysis, interpretation and revision has been for me a unique, inspiring learning experience.

If she has a problem in her work as a scientist, it may be

related to her participation in the "helping professions." So eager is she to be sure that her readers understand that Sephardim should be better known for their characteristics and for the accomplishments of their leaders, that she finds it hard to stop giving information. She is justified in this, because the story she tells, of a people who have contributed so much during their own golden age in medieval Spain and who still contribute to the cultural, commercial and educational progress of America and the world, has no end. So why should she make an ending?

As a scientific study, Mizrahi's dissertation ranks in the upper group of those with which I am pleased to have been associated. It stands as peer to many works that have been published and, we hope, may soon enjoy that status.

Read it--you'll like it!

Philip Merrifield, Ph.D.
Professor of Applied Psychology
New York University

Acknowledgments

The research and writing of <u>The Sources of Diversity in Sephardim</u>* was a long journey, a challenge I could not have completed alone. I want to thank my Committee members: first, my Committee Chairman and Advisor, Dr. Martin Hamburger, for his special electricity and solicitous support. I deeply appreciate the inspiration, career impetus, care, and concern he provided in many ways over the last thirteen years. I owe more than thanks to Dr. Philip Merrifield whose hand is throughout every phase of this dissertation. Professor Merrifield gave of his time beyond all reasonable expectation. I will be forever indebted to him for his patience, generosity, and brilliant guidance. To Dr. Morris I. Stein, I extend my sincerest thanks for his ideas and encouragement.

To this I add admiration to the scholars in the Sephardic community who gave of their time and expertise without financial remuneration. I am grateful to the six member panel who cooperated with the time consuming chore of validating cultural characteristics and who were otherwise "on call" for their expertise. They are: David F. Altabe, Associate Professor; Rachel Dalven, Ph.D., Professor Emeritus; Joseph Papo, MSW; Rabbi M. Mitchell Serels, Ph.D. Candidate; Henry Toledano, Ph.D., Associate Professor; and, especially, The Haham Rabbi Solomon Gaon, Ph.D., Chief of the World Sephardi Foundation. During the eleven years of the course of the study, upon being frequently called, Rabbi Gaon's response was always the same--informative, encouraging and, especially, kind. It was he and Rabbi M. Mitchell Serels who made available Yeshiva University's comprehensive mailing list for use in this research. Also, my gratitude goes to Rabbi Malcolm Stern, D.H.L., D.D., President of the Jewish Historical Society, who provided a listing of descendants of the Founding Father families.

*Dissertation

I am especially grateful to the 703 Sephardic individuals who took the time to complete a detailed eight page mailed questionnaire. Many wrote encouraging notes in the margins and sent letters or cards. My special thanks to Hayyim Cohen, Ph.D., the first to say "Do it!", and my warm appreciation to Eze Bashy, Rabbi Ben Haim, Michael H. Cardozo, Esther Gold, Richard Hansen, Ph.D., Marilyn Levy, Rabbi Arnold B. Marans, Eli Mizrahi, Harry Morris, Bernard Ouziel, Victor Sanua, Ph.D., Joseph A. D. Sutton, and Vicki Tamir. Ora Ezrachi, computer consultant, gave her ingenuity and long hard hours to an extremely complex data base. My deepest thanks to Essie Borden for her efficient, flying-typing-fingers, her unruffled accuracy and, for thinking of everything. And, to Louise Prado, my understanding and generous boss.

Finally, these acknowledgments would not be complete without mention of friends and family who touched this research in different ways.

Our dearest friend, the late journalist and author, Paul Hoffman, edited early drafts of the first two chapters with impeccable grammatical standards and fierce insistence on clarity. Had he lived, the final document would be better written;

Margaret R. Wolf, wise friend and counselor, whose ideas and insight helped so much in the early stages of the study;

Dr. Nina R. Lief, who, in ways she best understands, steadfastly guided me and preserved my sanity during frenetic hours on this academic journey;

Millicent Schoenbaum, Barbara Sirkin, and Alice Snyder, loyal friends, whose concern and support made such a difference;

Robert B. Fleck, for his genealogical expertise and for helping to stuff and sort nearly 5,000 envelopes!;

My cousin, the late David E. Mizrahi, of Geneva, who in his visits to New York would remind me of my Sephardic heritage as much through his illustrious style as through his words;

My father, the late Selim D. Mizrahi, of Damascus, from whom I acquired a sense of the moral imperative. My love for this honorable man of tradition and principle provided me with my purpose in undertaking the study;

My Ashkenaze mother, Rose M. Mizrahi, the first to teach me the good qualities of the Sephardim. Out of loving marital loyalty, and with competence and style, she maintained the Sephardic tradition in my childhood home;

Our fifteen year old son, Bruce, was a strong impetus for me to complete the study, so that I could share with him the very valuable information I learned about his Sephardic American heritage; and he provided perceptive critiques and computer expertise;

My husband, E. Bruce Haggerty, friend and partner at every turn. He lugged the bags, tolerated, read, and edited, but most of all, I will not forget that it was he who insisted that the decision to finish was not negotiable.

I wanted to learn about the complexity of the Sephardic experience in America and share what I learned. Although it was a stressful and difficult project, I don't regret the effort because of the knowledge I gained. I hope that it will prove to be of value to others.

A special acknowledgment is due to Philip Merrifield who, after his professorial obligations were done, served for many hours as a friend in assisting with the revisions needed to produce the present document from the dissertation.

Introduction

The impetus for this research began in the 1970's, when I was thinking of a topic for my doctoral thesis. At the time, there was very little information available to the general American public about Sephardic Jewry. In my personal experience, I met with total ignorance of their existence almost always, confusion, or on occasion an offensive misperception about them.

From my earliest childhood, I felt admiration and love for my Sephardic father, Selim D. Mizrahi, and pride in being part of his family. They were people of culture and substance. His mother was from the Austrian branch of the old and aristocratic DePicciotto family. His father was an Iranian physician who settled in Damascus and adopted the name of Mizrahi. My father was intelligent, well educated, kind and decent. At the age of 22, in Damascus, he started the first electrical company in Syria. At about that time, he began his lifelong pattern of world travel--to Europe, the Orient, and America. In the 1920's and 30's, he collected, exhibited and sold fine objets d'art, such as ivory, jade, and rose quartz. He had exquisite taste and a natural eye and love for things of beauty and value. He was established financially and socially in Europe before he settled in America, from Brussels, in 1938 at the age of 40. My mother, Rose Musikantow Mizrahi, was very young when she married (nineteen). She is Ashkenaze and American born, but out of love and respect for her husband, adopted many of his ways.

Selim Mizrahi was concerned with the well being of the Sephardic community in Los Angeles, and gave of his time and energies to help structure a charitable, social and religious organization of Sephardic businessmen. What I remember and admired most about him were his high moral and ethical standards, including high standards of honesty in his dealings with others.

While I was growing up, and as an adult, I observed both an extraordinary range of diversity and at the same time a strong communality amongst American Sephardim. The diversity seemed related in part to country and city of origin, socioeconomic status at the time of arrival to America, and time of immigration to America. Yet, despite these enormous differences, all considered themselves Sephardic, were united by a common liturgy, shared a group feeling and held similar traditions and life perspective. And, all Sephardim are strangers to the predominant culture of American Jewry, which is that of the originally German or Yiddish speaking Ashkenazim.

When many people I met assumed that all American Jews were Ashkenazim, and even many of my friends did not comprehend the complexities of the American Sephardic group, I realized the need for information and research on this topic. I was dismayed by these many lacks of comprehension, especially inconsistent with my knowledge and feelings of pride about not only the prominent role of Sephardim in world and American history, but also about my father's distinguished family.

My father had strong convictions, and I am like him in this way. My dismay about the misinformation and lack of information was transmuted into academic action. As a doctoral student and as a Sephardic American, my goals were clear: to investigate, to learn, and to educate both Sephardim and other Americans. I believed it would be important to clarify the various misperceptions related to my background, not only for me personally but because more information about American Sephardim would have social value. If my doctoral research were successful, I would be able to provide information that would add to the mosaic of the development of America and enhance appreciation of the diversity that gave such strength to this nation. It might help the morale of American Sephardim and might be a contribution for everyone, because understanding differences is a first step in interchanging in a positive manner. Also, how people identify with their group and are culturally validated by others in the society has implications for self-concept, self-esteem and sense of belonging. This is true, of course, not only for Sephardim, but for people of all groups. One of the many interesting results of the study was the data that emerged showing that, while Sephardic respondents felt strongly about their heritage, they perceived equally strongly that non-Sephardim didn't know what that was (page 57).

Thus, this study evolved. It started with feelings and a desire to correct errors of omission and commission in the general pool of knowledge. The continuing motivation was learning, for my own interest and to meet the requirements for my doctorate, which is why the topic was approached as it was:

- learning more about the diversity and cohesiveness of Sephardic groups in America. For example, see discussions below of four major strains among American Sephardim (page 3), and two definitions of Sephardim (page 7);

- the search for a theoretical foundation for a definition of Jewish (Sephardic) Identity;

- developing, with expert help, a questionnaire to gather evidence pertaining to degree of Identity endorsed by each participant in the study;

- application of the powerful techniques of factor analysis and other statistics to provide a conversion of the questionnaire responses to usable numbers based on internal construct validation (whether the questionnaire measures what it was intended to assess);

- examination of the averages and ranges of the numerical evidence to see whether the measures of Identity varied amongst the Sephardic national groups, and to find the degree of cohesiveness (communality) amongst Sephardim as a larger group that can still be seen as distinct from Ashkenazim and non-Jews.

It should be clear to the reader that the following results and discussions are not advanced as complete information about Sephardic diversity and cohesiveness. The importance of identifying and understanding Sephardic diversity and unity was considered in my research in the context of developing a valid and reliable questionnaire and in exploring what attitudes and attributes combine to make up and define Sephardic Identity. I hope that my academic efforts, which document the breathtaking range of diversity and make more specific some of the communality, and which provide statistically valid and reliable guidelines will make a contribution to clarifying the misinformation and lack of information about my background, which I so often encountered and which dismayed me and ultimately provided the impetus to undertake this long journey. It would not have been completed save for the continuous support and patience of my sponsors at New York University, Rabbi Gaon, my friends, and my family.

Fig. 1. My father (far right) as a young man, with his brothers and other relatives in the family home courtyard--Damascus, 1929.

"I know nobody taught us any of this . . ."

--Sidney Zion, 1971

703 AMERICAN SEPHARDIM:
Diversity within Cohesiveness

When I began my research in the 1970's, there was a long-standing omission in both popular media and ethnic identity literature of the recognition of diverse subgroups within the Jewish American population. Among the few Americans who may have known about American Sephardic culture, many were confused by it, unaware that American Sephardim are extremely diverse. With regard to the omission of Sephardic Jews specifically, [in his New York Times review of Birmingham's (1971) The grandees] Sidney Zion reminisces about his youth in Passaic, New Jersey, where nothing of the presence of Sephardim on Columbus' ships or during Colonial or American Revolutionary War days was taught him either in public school or at the Hebrew school he attended for five years. "I know nobody taught us any of this ... because we were always on the lookout for Jewish heroes and we would have talked about it all the time" (New York Times, 4/18/71). Angel (1971) wrote that "When politicians want to attract Jewish voters, they drop Yiddish phrases into their campaign speeches, even when their audiences are Sephardic" (p. 5). And, even today, some use "Jewish" interchangeably with "Ashkenaze."

In America, Sephardim are a minority within a minority. They comprise only 3 percent of all Jews, who themselves are not even 3 percent of the total population. American Sephardic Identity, therefore, is embedded and buried under the general concept of Jewish Identity, which in America generally reflects the Ashkenaze tradition and culture. Ashkenazim are Jews who track their roots to Central or Eastern Europe and who were, originally, predominantly speakers of German or its derivative, Yiddish. And, there are the Sephardim. American Sephardim are a diverse and complex minority, though all are united by a strong group feeling and a common liturgy. Equally, all are strangers to the predominant culture of American Jewry, which is that of the originally German or Yiddish speaking Ashkenazim.

In my doctoral dissertation, <u>Sources of diversity in Sephardim</u> (1987), I explored Sephardic American Identity. Simon Herman's (1977) theory of Jewish Identity provided the theoretical framework upon which I designed the questionnaire. I designed an eight-page questionnaire, consisting of 80 open- and close-ended questions. This questionnaire required intensive preliminary research into the question "By which criteria can a particular cultural or ethnic group's identity be reliably and validly measured?" Approximately 5,000 questionnaires were distributed to Sephardim primarily in the New York-New Jersey area, with the addition of Early American Sephardim along the Eastern Seaboard from Washington to Boston. Seven hundred and three completed questionnaires were received from eight different Sephardic national subgroups: Bukharan (34), Egyptian (46), Greek (135), Iraqi (66), Moroccan (50), Syrian (131), Turkish (213), and Early American (28). To the best of my knowledge the figure of 703 individuals from eight different subgroups represents the biggest range of Sephardim ever sampled. I am greatly indebted to those of you in the Sephardic community who responded and am proud to share some of my findings with you through this document. Much precision in the analysis is sacrificed to its simplicity in this presentation. Detailed descriptions of techniques, outcomes and extensive presentations of the tabular results of the data analysis may be found in my dissertation (Mizrahi, 1987).

"The whole character and fortune of the
individual are affected by . . . the
perception of differences."
--Emerson, Nature: Addresses

1. FOUR MAJOR STRAINS
AMONG AMERICAN SEPHARDIM

Among the few Americans who may know about Sephardic
culture, many are confused about it, unaware that American
Sephardim are extremely diverse and include people of many
subcultures. One finds at least four major strains among
American Sephardim: (a) the aristocratic "Grandees" depicted by
Stephen Birmingham (1971), descendants of the "Founding Fathers
of American Jewry," who were the first Jewish cultural group to
settle in America and the dominant one for two hundred years;
(b) the second and third generation of the wave of impoverished
immigrants who arrived at the turn of the century, mostly from
Syria, also Turkey and Greece, of whom many--like other Jews and
other immigrants of that era--have since risen to the middle and
upper-middle classes; (c) a pre- and post-World War II influx of
middle and well-established upper class internationally oriented
business, professional, and banking people, mostly from
cosmopolitan centers such as Baghdad, Beyrouth, Cairo, Damascus, Elizabethville (Belgian Congo), Rome, Salisbury (Rhodesia),
and Teheran, who have maintained the same status in the New
World; and (d) a post-Suez (1956) tide predominantly of poor
people from Moslem nations--mostly Morocco but also in smaller
numbers from Egypt, Iraq and Bukhara--who could not
accommodate themselves in Israel and who arrived in the U.S. in
the last four decades. Some of those who arrived via Israel are
middle class, for example, many Bukharans (The Haham, Dr.

3

Solomon Gaon, personal communication, July 19, 1985). During this same period, Iraqis, Iranians and some Egyptians, some of whom have high financial and social position, arrived directly from their countries rather than via Israel.

Most writers on the subject refer to the three waves of Jewish immigration to America as Sephardic, German, and Russian, in that order. American Sephardim were the first. They comprised the American-Jewish leadership until 1848, when German-Ashkenazim became more numerous. The year 1905 marked the beginning of the Russian period, when Russian and Eastern-European Ashkenazim surpassed the Germans in number.

As the first Jewish group in America, Sephardim set the stage for later arriving Ashkenazim and Sephardim. Spanish and Portuguese Jews (some of whom became temporary Catholics at the time of the Inquisition and were called "Conversos" or "Marranos") sailed on Columbus' ships. The Western Sephardim were the first Jewish cultural group to settle in colonial America and the dominant one for 200 years. Twenty-three Sephardic Jews arrived in New Amsterdam in 1654, the starting point of Jewish community life in North America, and their cultural dominance in Jewish-American life persisted until about 1848. Most of the Sephardic Jews of colonial America were of the merchant or upper classes, arriving with financial security and maintaining it. Daniel Gomez developed the fur industry (his son employed John Jacob Astor). Haym Solomon bankrolled the American Revolution. Uriah Levy purchased and restored Monticello, and in 1792, members of the Shearith Israel Congregation were among the founders of the New York Stock Exchange. David Levi Peixotto helped organize the Republican Party in the early 1800s. With Paul Revere, Harmon Hendricks dominated the copper industry. Judah Benjamin served as Secretary of War and State in the Confederacy. The Nathans and several related old Sephardic families produced men and women of stature in every generation. Rabbi Gershon Seixas of Shearith Israel was the first spiritual

4

leader in America; Annie Nathan Meyer founded Barnard College; Benjamin Nathan Cardozo was a U.S. Supreme Court justice. As late as the early 20th century Sephardim were the only Jews admitted to such exclusive New York clubs as the Union and Knickerbocker. Baltzell referred to this first period of American Jewish history as the classic period of "aristocratic assimilation" and said that it continued until the early part of the 20th century, when caste barriers, based on religion, were erected (1966).

After 1830, Jewish immigration rose sharply--mostly poor Ashkenaze Jews from Bavaria who arrived with other German immigrants. Most German Jews began as peddlers, in contrast to the Sephardim of the previous period who came as merchants and entrepreneurs. The main characteristics of the German or second period of immigration were the relatively small numbers of German Jews (much larger than the Sephardim, but small in relation to the Russians who followed) and their wide dispersion throughout rural America.

The third wave of Jewish immigration to America began in 1880 with the great influx of Eastern-European Ashkenazim. By 1905 there were more Russian than German Jews in America. The Russian immigrants went mainly to the large Eastern cities and most of them were extremely poor.

During this turn-of-the-century third, or Eastern-European, period of Jewish immigration, Levantine Sephardim began coming to America. There is a cultural distinction between the Western "founding father" Sephardim of colonial days and the Levantine Sephardim who came in the 20th century. Levantine Sephardim included both Spanish and Portuguese Jews exiled to North Africa and the eastern Mediterranean in 1492 and Jews who had been in the eastern Mediterranean since biblical times. The majority of Levantine Sephardim came to America in the late 19th and 20th centuries. They arrived under quite different circumstances from the "founding fathers"--some refugees from Turkey, North Africa,

5

the Balkans, and other Mediterranean countries. Many felt isolated--from both the predominantly European Christian Americans and from the American Jewish communities, which, for the most part, were Ashkenaze and German or Yiddish speaking. Chopped liver was as alien to Sephardim as rolled grape leaves were to the Ashkenazim.

A smaller influx of Sephardim arrived from their threatened World War II European environment, largely middle and upper class international, professional, business, and banking people from such world centers as Baghdad, Beyrouth, Cairo, Damascus, Elizabethville, Rome, Salisbury (Rhodesia), and Teheran.

Finally, a post-Suez (1956) tide arrived from Moslem nations, mostly Morocco, but also Egypt, Iran, Iraq, and Bukhara. Many of these came via Israel; some, though not all, were poor. Some emigrated directly from their countries, such as the Iraqis, Iranians, and some Egyptians, and, in addition, were quite wealthy.

For numerous reasons, including relatively small size, difficulty of access, and relatively recent arrival, there has not been much academic research on the late 19th and 20th century arriving Sephardic groups. There has been scattered research, often with small size or homogeneous sample groups, not large or diverse enough to show the heterogeneity of American Sephardim.

"If you wish to converse with me,
define your terms."

--Voltaire

2. TWO BASIC DEFINITIONS OF "SEPHARDIM"

There are two basic definitions of "Sephardim"--the restricted and the extended. Participants in this research were asked their opinion. Specifically, questionnaire item #17 asks, "Which groups of Jews do you think of as Sephardic?" Results and discussions appear on pages 29, 39, and 61 of this document. According to the restricted definition, "Sephardim" refers only to Spanish and Portuguese Jews. According to the extended, it refers to Jews who follow, in the main, the Sephardic liturgy, customs, and lifestyle and who come from countries influenced by Islamic culture, including, but not limited to, Spain, Portugal, Greece, Iran, Iraq, Syria, Lebanon, Egypt, Turkey, the Balkan states, North Africa, the Isle of Rhodes, Bukhara, and Afghanistan. The extended definition, rather than the restricted, is used by the vast majority of Sephardim and by most Sephardic organizations, including the American Sephardic Foundation and the Sephardic Studies Program at Yeshiva University. It was adopted at a symposium on Sephardism sponsored by the American Jewish Committee (American Jewish Committee, 1978).

Despite the widespread scholarly and popular usage of the extended definition, some Sephardim feel that "Sephardic" should be used restrictively--to mean only Iberian Jews. The reasons include pride of lineage, the desire to remain distinct, and emphasis on the differences rather than the similarities, among non-Ashkenaze national groups. Some Iraqi Jews feel great pride in their ancient heritage and claim that they are the direct

7

descendants of Babylonian Jewry--Jews of Israel who were taken into captivity by Nebuchadnezzar in the sixth century B.C. Unlike some of the Spanish Jews, they did not mix with other races. These Iraqi Jews believe that the distinction between their culture and the Spanish-Jewish should be preserved. Similarly, some Syrian and Persian Jews believe that "Sephardic" should be restricted to Iberian Jews because of their pride in ancient Syrian and Persian history. Syrian and Persian Jewry dates back to early migrations into those countries. Persian Jews, some of whose Jewish lineage is even older than the Babylonian Iraqis', are descendants of Jews from the Assyrian conquest of Israel in the ninth century B.C.

Some Jews who speak Judeo-Spanish (sometimes called "Ladino," though technically the term refers only to biblical translation) prefer the restricted definition, but for reasons different from those of the Iraqis, Syrians, and Persians. Some Judeo-Spanish-speaking Jews, who mostly come from Turkey and the Balkan states, believe that their culture is the true remnant of the glorious pre-Inquisition Iberian Jewry's and should be preserved distinct from non-Judeo-Spanish-speaking Jewish communities, like the North African Jews in Israel who are sometimes referred to as the "Black Panthers." The historic rationale for this is the belief that of the 400,000 to 600,000 Jews expelled from Spain and Portugal during the Inquisition in the 14th through 16th centuries, the vast majority went to the eastern coast of the Ottoman Empire--now Turkey and the Balkan states.

According to Rabbi Gaon, a well-known expert on Sephardism, a few people believe that "Sephardim" should be further restricted to those Spanish and Portuguese Jews who went to such countries as England and Holland and not confused with those who went to Turkey and the Balkan states. The reason is that the culture of the Spanish Jews who relocated to the Turkish-Balkan countries was heavily influenced by local customs, while those who migrated to Western Europe or South America preserved the Spanish culture and language (Rabbi Gaon, personal communication, 1981).

Users of the extended definition believe that there are unifying characteristics strong enough to justify use of "Sephardim" to mean both Iberian and Levantine Jewry. Joseph N. Papo (1987) notes Professor Jose Faur's concern about defining Sephardim solely on the basis of origin. Faur's (1972) apprehension is that such an approach might lead to the atomization of Sephardi group consciousness and thus may undermine their feeling of being a part of the Jewish people. According to Rabbi Gaon (1981), in the strictest sense, "Sephardim" has meant Iberian Jewry, but today it should be used in a wider and extended perspective. The rationale is that when the Jewish exiles left Spain, they scattered and not all took a direct path to Turkey and the Balkan states.

The Jews expelled from Iberia during the 14th through 16th centuries can be subdivided. Many went directly to the eastern coast of the Ottoman Empire and stayed there through four centuries. They are now referred to as Judeo-Spanish-speaking Turkish Jews. But many did not follow such a direct path. Some went to North Africa--about 80% to Morocco--and others to Italy and Syria. Tamir remarked that it is not known where all the expelled Spanish Jews went: some ended up in Bulgaria (Tamir, 1979). There were also some Spanish and Portuguese Jews who remained in Iberia and became crypto-Jews (Marranos), but who later went to Amsterdam and London and then, in the colonial period, to North America.

All these groups are really Sephardic, even though they scattered during the Inquisition and even though some became assimilated into the native Jewish populations they found upon migration. A map appears on the following page showing the waves of Sephardi emigration from Spain and Portugal after the Inquisition of 1492 (Encyclopaedia Judaica Jerusalem, 1972). It was mainly those who went to the Ottoman Empire, now Turkey,

9

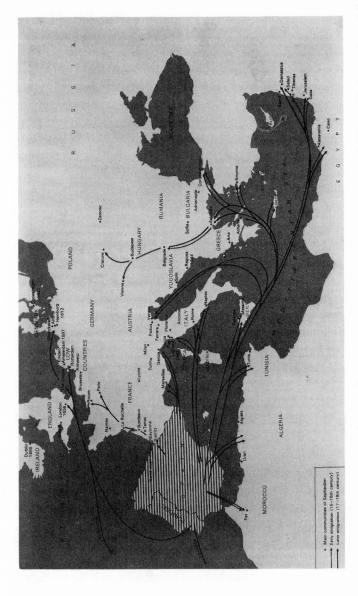

Fig. 2. Waves of Sephardi emigration from Spain and Portugal after the expulsion of 1492, with dates of establishment of new comunities where known. (H. Bainart) Courtesy of Encyclopaedia Judaica, Keter Publishing House, 1972.

who preserved the Spanish language, although the original Spanish changed into Judeo-Spanish (Ladino) through the influence of the local Turkish culture. Over the centuries, these Jews began to mix with the Turks and, according to Rabbi Gaon (1981), their Spanish became a "bit corrupted."

Direct Spanish lineage is even more difficult to trace for the Syrian Jews than for the Turkish, because the Turkish retained the language. At the beginning, the Syrian Jews mostly were Spanish Jews, but they learned Arabic and became absorbed into the native Jewish population, which included Jewish migrants from Iraq. Sutton noted that Jews were in Aleppo as early as the fourth century and obviously did not migrate during the Inquisition. On the other hand, the Spanish and Portuguese Jews who made their way to Syria from Salonika and Izmir in Turkey over the centuries were absorbed completely in the native Syrian Jewish population. Sutton concluded that some Jews always had lived in Syria and had no ancestral connection to Iberia, while others originated in Spain and Portugal and were swept to Syria by the fury of the Inquisition (Sutton, 1979). The same process of absorption occurred in North Africa and elsewhere.

Greece is a complex case in itself. Spanish Jews who went to Salonika and Mediterranean islands like Rhodes and DePalma, for the most part, absorbed the old Jewish communities that had been there since the time of the Second Temple, because of their stronger Spanish culture, their numbers, and their organizing power, according to Rabbi Gaon. Many Greek Jews, however, resisted this assimilation and, to the present day, speak Judeo-Greek, rather than Judeo-Spanish. According to Morris Yomtov, past president of the Janina Brotherhood (Yomtov, 1978), the Janina Greek Jews always had been Sephardic and in 1492, when Spanish Jews came to the Mediterranean islands, Sephardic Jews were there already, perhaps having migrated to Turkey from Israel. In 1492, at the same time as the Inquisition in Spain, there was a civil war and Turkey was split into Turkey and Greece.

11

According to Yomtov, some Greek Jews, who as Turkish Jews might have spoken Spanish, adopted Greek, which later became Judeo-Greek. Although they did not speak Spanish or Judeo-Spanish and never were victims of the Inquisition, they retained Sephardic culture, liturgy, and lifestyle.

Muslim culture also heavily influenced Spanish Jews. According to Rabbi Gaon, until 200 years before the Inquisition--and even after--Spanish Jews spoke Arabic and much of their writing and commerce was in Arabic, not Spanish. The major portion of the work of famous Spanish Jews like Maimonides, Halevi, and Ibn-Gabriel was in Arabic and only later translated into Hebrew. Even after 1492 many of the expelled Spanish Jews who went to Salonika continued to speak Arabic. Sutton explained that Spanish Sephardim were descended from Middle-Easterners: "They are revealed to have originated in the Middle-East; they had come in stages from Egypt, Baghdad, North Africa, Palestine and Syria ... In effect, Jewish Spain was merely an extension of the Middle-East" (1976, pp. 251-252)

Further clouding the issue is the appearance in the Bible of the words "Sephar" and "Sepharad" (Genesis 10:30 and Obadiah 1:20), meaning "north" or "east"--perhaps Mesopotamia or Armenia, although the land of Sepharad commonly is considered to be Spain.

In early 20th century America and contemporary Israel Levantine Sephardim are referred to as "oriental," but the term is considered pejorative by many Sephardim because it denies their legitimate Sephardism and falsely suggests a connection with the Far East.

12

"Nothing has such power to broaden the mind
as the ability to investigate systematically and
truly all that comes under thy observations
in life."
--Marcus Aurelius, Meditations, Bk. iii

3. BEGINNING: METHODS

Stated briefly, my goal was to gather evidence on
Sephardim's feelings of identity as Sephardim, in contemporary
America. I had come to believe that Sephardim had strong
national group feelings, so I hoped to be able to demonstrate two
levels of identity, corresponding to being Sephardic and, for
example, being Syrian.

In academic research, strong emphasis is placed on the
theoretical basis of how knowledge is organized for presentation,
that is, what general principles and ideas help tie together the
many facts available. It didn't take long to discover that there was
no existing theory of Sephardic national identity; this pleased me,
in a way, because it meant that my belief was perhaps a new
insight, or at least one that had been explored very little by others.
I did find useful the theories of identity based on other
recognizable groups which I had known about from my long
previous study of sociology and human relations; as a part of that
broad field of literature, the theoretical writings on Jewish Identity
by Zak (1972), Sandberg (1974), Dashefsky (1975), Driedger
(1976), Parmi-Tonu (1976), Cohen (1977), Hewitt (1980) and
Himmelfarb (1980) were not only of great interest but provided
some clues as to how I should best proceed.

13

My Proposal: A Three-Criteria Concept of Sephardic Identity Based on Simon Herman's Two-Criteria Theory of Jewish Identity

Nearly all Jewish and ethnic identity theorists stress that group identity is complex and multi-dimensional. An individual's sense of identity as a Jew, an American or a Sephardi consists not only of his typically religious or ethnic behaviors, but also his feelings and attitudes toward the group and the subgroups within it. In my research, I explored whether a three-criteria approach to Sephardic Identity would serve as a beginning definition. I explored Sephardic Identity as comprised of:
1) Alignment--or the way Sephardim align themselves with other Sephardim; (2) Adherence--or the extent to which Sephardim place value on and behave in "typically" Sephardic ways; and (3) Affinity--or the sense of special closeness Sephardim feel towards their particular national Sephardic subgroup (e.g., Turkish or Early American), when compared with the general Sephardic group and non-Sephardim. A detailed discussion and review of past Jewish and Ethnic Identity literature appears in the dissertation itself (Mizrahi, 1987). I designed the questionnaire used in this research with the purpose of obtaining information about the feasibility of this three-criteria approach to understanding Sephardic Identity.

The most useful theory I found upon which to design my own questionnaire was Simon Herman's classic work on Jewish Identity (1977). Herman concluded that two aspects of Jewish Identity had to be considered functionally separate: he called these Alignment and Adherence. (By functionally separate, he meant, as most social scientists would, that information about one of these aspects tells less than there is to know about the person being described--both are necessary in a description because the information they convey is different.) Herman defines Alignment as the ways that Jews see themselves as members of the Jewish Community in general, regardless of separations in time and geography, and also the way they see themselves as separate from

14

other, non-Jewish groups and individuals. By Adherence, he means the ways and degrees to which the individual lives daily by various rules, such as eating certain foods, attendance at religious services, and valuing highly certain behaviors towards other members of the group.

For my study, I adopted these guidelines, Alignment and Adherence, and adapted them to the definition of Sephardic Identity. By Alignment, I mean the degree to which Sephardim see themselves as members of the Sephardic Community; emphasizing aspects of Sephardic history and location; regarding themselves as separate from other Jewish groups, as well as from non-Jewish groups. By Adherence, I mean the ways in which Sephardim in their daily lives express their Sephardic Identity through typically Sephardic behaviors. In addition, I wanted to obtain evidence for my belief in national clusters within the Sephardic Community: this aspect I called Affinity. Thus, the theoretical orientation provides three strands on which three different aspects of Sephardic Identity may be based. As an analogy, we may think of three strands which may be braided into a single plait. (See Diagram of Three Criteria, p. 70, Fig. 3.)

Statistics as Needed

Because I decided to base my conclusions on averages rather than on individual cases, I decided to develop an extensive questionnaire rather than a plan for interviews of individual Sephardim. This approach made it necessary to use statistical analysis, rather than just pooling my opinions and impressions. The values of a statistical approach are not widely understood, and the techniques are sometimes maligned as "trickery." While it is possible, as with many techniques, to use them incorrectly to get more desirable results, I used "standard operating procedures" for this field of study; besides, my sponsoring professors are very conservative, so I could not have gone too far astray without their restraining me.

I'll be using statistics in three ways in this report: to tell us how reliable the questionnaire is; to tell us whether the three aspects of Sephardic Identity are separate, or whether we can just consider them as one thing; to tell us whether the degrees of Alignment, Adherence and Affinity reported by members of different national groups are different. Each of these will require a slightly different technique, so I'll comment on them as we go along.

Designing the Questionnaire

I had been pondering the questions I've been discussing, but I knew I needed some specific assistance. In my research design class, I asked, "How do you decide what specific questions to include in a questionnaire?" My professor answered, "It depends on what larger questions are to be answered. Wherever you can, use expert opinion about the area of the questions." Later, in his office, we discussed in greater detail how the Sephardic culture differed from other Jewish culture, and the possibility of getting expert opinion.

I needed first to find out what the literature and experts said were the typically Sephardic behaviors, in order to determine whether (and how much) Sephardim adhere to them (Criterion 2: Adherence). A major set of questions would be developed based on this complex and extensive but important preliminary research. My strategy was to work in two directions. I would ask experts to suggest various characteristics as typically Sephardic, and I would search the literature on Sephardim for references to such specific characteristics. The computer search facility through NYU's Bobst Library was very helpful in locating references, from which I selected 40 for further consideration. Meanwhile, I had asked community leaders to nominate experts to make the judgments I needed; six of those nominated agreed to help and are cited in my Acknowledgments, above, and in Appendix A. Their contributions were of great value. Not only did they judge every characteristic on the scale of 5 (extremely typical) through 1 (not typical), but they suggested an additional 14 characteristics. They then judged those 14, plus another 7 suggested from other sources--a total of 61. The full listing of 61 characteristics and the experts' consensual rating of degree of typicality appear in Appendix A of this book. Thirty-one characteristics, of the 60, survived the experts' rating for typicality of Sephardic culture. These 31 characteristics were transformed into questionnaire items. The 31 characteristics, the degree of typicality given by the experts and the degree of importance given by the 703 Sephardim who completed questionnaires appear on page 49 of this document.

Selection of Items

To select the characteristics suitable for the questionnaire, we decided that the six judges should agree within 2 points that a characteristic was typical, and that the average of the six ratings had to indicate the consensus that the item was "typical, very typical, or extremely typical". For example, if five judges thought a characteristic was "very typical" and one thought it "not typical" it was not used because the spread was more than 2 points (4 vs. 1); on the other hand, if four thought it typical and one thought it extremely typical, it would be used.

As the final selection of typical items was being made, we recognized our first evidence that my choice of Herman as a major referent had been on the right track. Most of the items the experts thought were typical or more characteristic of Sephardim were good examples either of Herman's categories of Alignment or Adherence, or of what I planned to call the aspect of Affinity.

Obtaining Individual Attitude Measures

Each participant in the study was to indicate the extent to which each characteristic was important in his daily life. The number of points he received for his response was high if he thought an extremely typical characteristic was very important; if he thought that characteristic was of less importance, he would receive fewer points. His total degree of Adherence was indicated by the sum of the points received for all the characteristics assigned to Adherence. Similarly, his degree of Alignment and Affinity were computed as the sum of points from the characteristic behaviors participants reported.

Here are some examples of behaviors and beliefs related to the three criteria:

Alignment #34a Do you feel your hopes and aspirations are bound up with the hopes and aspirations of all Sephardim? (Yes to No on a five-point scale)

Adherence #79 One must never disrespect one's parents. (Agree Strongly to Disagree Strongly on a five-point scale)

Affinity #32b To what extent do you feel close to Sephardim of your own national group? (Extremely Close to Not Close on a five-point scale)

At last, 62 items were ready for inclusion in the questionnaire. They were from several sources: the splendid efforts of the Sephardic experts; my own ideas of national group feeling; and, consistency with Herman's findings. To aid in future interpretation of the responses, we added questions dealing appropriately with occupation, income, sex, age, family history, and the like. I was ready to collect the data!

18

Participants in the Survey

Who should be asked to participate? Joel (2:28) tells us, "Your old men shall dream dreams, your young men shall see visions." Young women, too: my aspirations rose to include a national survey, representative of Sephardim from all national groups from all parts of the United States; it would have been wonderful. But the cost of contacting such a population, selecting individuals from it according to scientific principles, and the postage and printing, and so on, would be very great.

Realistically, I defined the target population as members of the Sephardic Community with major family ties to the greater New York City area. In the actual data collection, 92% of those to whom the questionnaire was sent were on the mailing list of the Sephardic Studies Program of Yeshiva University; for the rest, I relied on personal knowledge of established nation-oriented groups of Sephardim in the area. A total of 4,874 questionnaires were distributed; most were mailed in January, 1981, but distribution through various channels continued through October 1981.

The Number of Respondents

In most surveys of this kind, the number of responses seems to average about 16% of the number sent out. Because I had to consider the statistical procedures to come, I decided that I needed to get at least 27 responders from a national group in order to justify including that national subgroup in the study. By observing both guidelines, I decided to close the data collection late in 1981 after 795 questionnaires had been returned. After the inevitable attrition due to incomplete responses, the number of usable questionnaires was 703, still a net response rate of 14%. This is in some disproportion in regard to relative size of the actual nation-oriented groups. The sample may still be unbiased, in that all respondents would have had to be relatively active members of a community in order to have been sent a questionnaire, and the act of response itself is evidence of interest in communal characteristics. It's important to tell you that Rabbi Gaon thought (personal communication, 1981) that the response rate was exceptionally high for Sephardim, who tend to guard and promote their privacy. Those who came forth by responding show their membership in the population I was trying to learn more about. As you will recall, the questionnaire was anonymous, so we are unable to say anything about rates of response by national group.

Demographic Characteristics of Respondents

In Tables 1 through 6 (pages 34-39 below), you may find the demographic characteristics of those in the sample we obtained. Of the 703 participants, 69% were female, more than half were born in the United States, more than half had completed four years or more of college, 38% reported incomes of $30,000 (1981 dollars) or more, and almost three-fourths reported themselves as either postgraduate or professional, or holding proprietary positions in business. They were from eight national groups: Bukharan (34), Egyptian (46), Greek (135), Iraqi (66), Moroccan (50), Syrian (131), Turkish (213), and Early American (28). More about demographic characteristics of respondents appears under Results beginning on page 32 of this summary.

Assessing Individual Attitudes towards Sephardic Identity

After the responses to the questionnaires had been converted to points by the steps described above, I was once again ready to consider whether the three aspects of Sephardic Identity were actually separate. The statistical answer to this kind of question involves the procedure called factor analysis. This

20

procedure was first developed to study achievement and "intelligence," and is widely used in studies of attitude and other aspects of personality. It provides a way of grouping items with regard to clusters of responses; if most participants respond consistently to a group of items, a numerical index of the degree of clustering will be high. Consistency of response to two items, for example, means that those persons who agree on the importance of one behavior will also find the other behavior important, and that those persons who believe that the first behavior is unimportant will also believe the second is unimportant. An inconsistent response would be one in which some of those who think the first is important think the second is also important, and some do not, and conversely. In other words, consistent responses are evidence for our belief in a single statistical factor, while inconsistent responses suggest that, at the statistical level of reasoning, we need more than one factor to describe, numerically, the differences between participants' responses.

Having come to a statistical decision from the quantitative analysis, we need to look at the kinds of behavior indicated by each item in a cluster to decide which aspect of behavior is represented by that cluster. Then we can use the attitudes reflected in each cluster as more general labels for describing the participants in the study. Our hope is that the clusters of items we assigned to each of the three aspects are quite similar to the clusters of items which come together statistically as factors. We anticipated that there would be a statistically supportable cluster of items corresponding to Alignment, another to Adherence, and a third to Affinity.

Construct Validation Theory

Construct validation theory evolved in the 1950s when an attempt was made to set forth quality standards for commercially published tests, based on a broader view of validity than previously

21

held. A joint committee of representatives from the American Psychological Association and the American Education Research Association was charged with the task of defining this broader view, though validity always means the degree to which an instrument measures the label that is put upon it. It is a characteristic of the instrument. The Committee stated as explicitly as it could what validating research should be completed before a test is widely distributed. The Committee developed recommendations applicable to various types and uses of tests, and distinguished three forms of validity--criterion related, content, and construct. The Committee's report in the 1950s was reissued with some extensions by the American Psychological Association in 1974. This terminology was generally accepted and continues to be in use today.

First of all, a construct is an a priori part of theory; it is "constructed out of the investigator's experience and knowledge." The construct becomes established--accepted into the set of constructs--if it meets certain qualifications, e.g., being separate from other constructs. The purpose of devising and validating an instrument that measures a particular construct is so that one can have confidence in the construct's place in theory. Each construct belongs to and explicates a theory. It is an intermediate step, often called a building block of a theory. It is part of the transition from the abstract theoretical statement to the actual measure of behavior. In the present study, the major construct is Sephardic Identity. There are three subconstructs, at different levels of generality: Criterion 1, Criterion 2, and Affinity. In the present study, the construct validity of relevant parts of the Sephardic Identity Survey is investigated.

The key to construct validity is that it refers to the validation of a measure of a construct. According to Kerlinger (1973, p. 456):

Construct validity is one of the most significant

22

advances of modern measurement theory and practice. It is a significant advance because it unites psychometric notions with theoretical notions . . . it is not simply a question of validating a test.

Criteria for Construct Validity

Construct validity differs from other types of validity in its preoccupation with theory, theoretical constructs, and scientific empirical inquiry involving the testing of hypothesized relations (Kerlinger, p. 462). The nugget of construct validation is when

> . . . the test developed (or some later writer) proposes a certain interpretative construct, explains at greater or lesser length what the construct means, and offers some evidence that persons scoring high on the test also exhibit other behavior associated with the construct. (Cronbach, 1971, p. 465)

So, the construct is hypothesized as an aspect of individual differences. It is hypothesized that a person who has this construct should behave in certain ways that are different from someone who does not have the construct. Construct validity addresses the question of whether a test validly dsecribes individuals in terms of the construct " . . . together with other information about him and in various situations" (Cronbach, 1971, p. 446).

Theory evolves by the test developer first proposing a certain set of related constructs then discussing the meaning of each and showing that he has a test that is construct valid, i.e., it is a valid measure of each construct. But, in the continuing interpretation of a test, its construct validity is challenged over and over again. This challenge consists of proposing another construct or constructs which might account for the behavior exhibited on the test.

For a test to have construct validity, it must focus as closely as possible on the construct; this means that the responses elicited by the test or questionnaire items must be internally consistent or--to borrow a term from factor analysis--univocal. This is the same requirement that is imposed for internal-consistency reliable, so we may say that to have construct validity, the score that is to be interpreted as a measure of that construct must first be reliable. It is frequently the case that a questionnaire, once developed, turns out to require experience or knowledge that may not be directly related to the construct that is its intended focus. Individual differences in these aspects, e.g., experience with cultural characteristics, vocabulary, language structure used in asking questions, will appear to contribute to the reliability of the test, if they pervade many of the questions, but they will cloud the validity of the score for the construct. That is, a person may get a high score if he understands the questions and endorses the attitudes represented; but he may get a low score even if he, too, endorses the attitudes but cannot say so because he doesn't understand the questions or has not had the necessary experiences.

Finally, when related constructs are being investigated, it is not unusual that a single questionnaire will contain responses that are valid for more than one construct. This situation is sometimes troublesome, but is difficult to avoid; it leads to correlations among measures of the constructs, but these correlations are part of the validity of the construct. In contrast, correlations arising from the intrusive aspects mentioned earlier are not part of the validity, and thus should be minimized in the construction of the questionnaire. While high reliability is necessary for high validity, it does not guarantee it. One needs to appeal to expert judgments and to external correlates of the score to fully establish construct validity. If the pattern of correlations among responses conforms to what experts in the theoretical aspects of the construct/theory would expect, confidence in construct validity is strengthened. If the correlations are not as expected, one has to make a choice between the validity of the responses and the opinions of the experts.

Factor Analysis as a Method of Construct Validation

Factor analysis provides factorial validity for the test items, which is strong internal evidence for the similarity of the items to each other. The construct validity of a test depends almost entirely on the correlations of the items with other measures. Factor analysis is used to establish that there is a dimension on which individuals differ. Factorial validity is related to construct validity through (a) the opinions of experts regarding the relevance to the construct of items loading high on the factor, (b) the correlations of factor scores to scores on other known or hypothesized measures of the construct, and (c) the correlation of factor scores in expected ways with other characteristics of the respondents. According to Kerlinger (1973, p. 468),

Factor analysis is perhaps the most powerful method of construct validation . . . a method for reducing a large number of measures to a smaller number called factors by discovering which ones "go together"--measure the same thing--and the relations between the clusters of measures that go together.

This means items are devised that logically should measure aspects of the construct and the investigator then examines if in fact they do. First, the items can be said to measure something if he gets reliable individual differences from them. The investigator then takes another set of items and sees if they also measure reliable individual differences. Then in order for the investigator to say that they are both measures of the same construct, they must correlate highly with each other; the chances are that what it is that they are jointly measuring is the construct that he had in mind when the items were developed. This is a process of testing conjectures. The more items that can be gathered to measure the same construct, the more confident one can feel that a reliable and generalizable measure of the construct has been achieved. The correlations between measures ascribed to the same construct indicate the degree of construct validity of the measures. "Factor analysis tells us, what measures measure the same thing and to what extent they measure what they measure" (1973, Kerlinger, p. 468). Factor analysis is a form of correlation-ship analysis of the measure with other measures and is based on the idea that one way to learn about a construct is to know both its correlates and its non-correlates.

In the present study, a factor analysis was used to establish that there is a construct which can be called Sephardic Identity, according to which individuals differ. For example, we can identify Criterion 1 items by reference to Herman's theory. We arrive at the decision of whether that set of items has internal consistency through factor analysis. Factor analysis is used as a psychometric justification for finding out something about theory. It leads us to finding out how much of the test variance is attributable to each of a number of constructs, including both the intended construct and the impurities (Cronbach, 1971, p. 469).

"Jewish life should be viewed in its totality, as one field, i.e., as a constellation of inter-dependent factors."

--Simon Herman (based on Lewin), 1977

4. RESULTS

After a description of the data analysis (including a statement about reliability and validity of the findings), the results will be presented in the following order:

- how respondents define "Sephardim",

- theory of Sephardic Identity,

- diversity,

- cohesiveness,

- assimilation?

- Sephardic personality: a minority within a minority.

Data Analysis

The analysis of questionnaire responses was carried out at the New York University Academic Computing Facility. Computer programs were taken from the Statistical Package for the Social Sciences (SPSS). Initially, the number of respondents answering each item in each possible way was tabulated and the results inspected to assure that subsequent data analysis would be based on statistically appropriate input. Demographic data also were processed using the frequency distribution programs, and crosstabulations. The primary tool for determining the psychological, attitudinal ways the respondents differed was factor analysis; this complex technique is based on correlations, i.e., whether a particular response to one question gives a strong indication of that individual's response to another question. This technique is invaluable in investigating questions regarding the different aspects of Sephardic Identity. To answer the author's questions about differences between groups of Sephardim differing in national origin, the major technique used was analysis-of-variance; this statistical approach compares the amount of difference among members of a group with the size of the difference between the average of that group and some other group. Further details of procedures and outcomes may be found elsewhere (Mizrahi, 1987; SPSS, 1975, 1981).

Reliability of the Findings

The reliabilities of the three measures we developed are between .70 and .80; in this area of study, 1.0 is the highest possible value for reliability. In terms of the 5-point scale used for the responses, this level of reliability means that a person's scores on two questionnaire items belonging to the same aspect would not differ by more than half a point, in three out of four comparisons of such scores. In simpler terms, we can count on these responses as being pretty much what we would get if we asked again.

Validity of the Findings

Because this summary is intended for the general reader, only brief mention is made here of the issue of validity. However, the work done toward validating the three facets of Sephardic Identity (Alignment, Adherence and Affinity) and defining them pervades the entire dissertation in great detail. In brief, this research followed three procedures for establishing construct validity:

First: logical (content validity) set up by experts' opinions;
Second: factorial validity confirmed by factor analysis for Herman's Alignment and Adherence; four aspects of Affinity supported by correlational analysis;
Third: "known group" method confirmed by differences in national group, as expected.

Based on the similarity of the patterns of questionnaire items expected to assess the three facets of Sephardic Identity and the actual patterns resulting from the factor analysis, we can rest comfortably in the belief that the "construct" validity of the results is sufficiently high to warrant our going ahead with the rest of the investigation. The issue of "predictive" validity, or what the findings from the factor analysis can tell us about different attitudes among national groups, will be presented in a later section (p. 40).

How Respondents Define "Sephardim"

The results of open-ended questionnaire item #17, which asked the respondent which groups of Jews he thinks of as Sephardic, suggest differences of understanding (or at least point of view) within the Sephardic group. Of those who answered the question (6% did not), fifty percent considered Sephardim to be those non-Ashkenazim who may or may not have direct Iberian ancestry but who follow Sephardic customs and liturgy; 30% restricted their definition of Sephardism to those of direct Iberian ancestry; and 20% reported themselves undecided or gave such amorphous answers that they could not be categorized.

The apparent lack of a clear-cut commonly accepted definition among Sephardim themselves (or at least those participating in this study) has implications not only for the study of Sephardic Identity per se, but for correlates to Sephardic Identity, such as self-esteem, self-concept, and sense of belonging. Responses from the various national groups are presented in Table 6 (page 39).

Theory of Sephardic Identity

Sephardic Identity Too Complex for Single Score: Three Facets Emerge

When we ask the question, "What is a Sephardi's attitude toward his Sephardism?", it would be reasonable to expect a simple "positive" or "negative" response. But that would ignore the complexity of human behavior, as well as the many aspects of Sephardism, or of any cultural pattern. The salient conclusion, most conservatively stated here, is that Sephardic Identity is multi-dimensional: at least three measures emerged in this research. It should be clear to the reader that the results are not advanced as complete information about Sephardic Identity. Statistical significance is conservatively interpreted to mean that the author has moved away from some baseline; there are reliable and valid relations among the proposed three criteria for Sephardic Identity. The development of a scale, in the psychometrically sound sense, will require some pruning of the current results and perhaps some newer revised items aimed at increasing reliability and validity. At the least, though, the author claims to be on track to the development of such a scale and to the further clarification of Sephardic Identity. (See Diagram of Three Criteria, p. 70, Fig. 3.)

Sephardic Identity is multi-dimensional; at least three measures emerged in this research. Each of these three measures is complex and composed of submeasures. For example, the first measure of a person's Sephardic Identity would be to ask how aligned he feels with other Sephardim--this set of questions is called "Alignment" in this study and constitutes Criterion I. However, Alignment is complex; to really find out how close or aligned a person feels to other Sephardim, one must ask Which Sephardim, Where and When? Thus, the Alignment criterion is broken down into submeasures such as "Do you feel close to Sephardim in the past?" (Alignment across time) and "Do you feel close to Sephardim in Israel?" (Alignment across space). The second criterion of Sephardic Identity is how much the person values characteristics considered "typically" Sephardic. The set of questions pertaining to it are called "Adherence to the characteristics." Measuring how much someone values a typical characteristic, however, involves an estimation of not only the degree of value the Sephardi places on something like eating typical food, but also the degree of typicality of that characteristic has to be factored in in order to get a more accurate measure of salience. It is too much to go into here, but details, including specifics of all criteria and subcriteria, may be found in the dissertation (Mizrahi, 1987, Appendices B, D, H and L).

In his investigation of Jewish attitudes toward their own identity, Herman proposed two ways to respond: with regard to Alignment, a sharing of ideas and beliefs with other Jews; and with regard to Adherence, a matter of behaving in conformity with accepted rules and procedures about family relationships, diet, and so forth. Because of my observation of the diversity within Sephardim, I proposed an additional way to respond: Affinity, or feeling of belongingness to one's own national subgroup, with the expectation that Affinity would be greater within groups of the same national origin than between Sephardim with differing national origins. The technique of factor analysis was applied to verify that the questions about Alignment were more closely related to themselves than to questions about Adherence or Affinity, and that those for Adherence were more closely intertwined than the questions for Alignment or Affinity, and that those questions dealing with Affinity were closer to each other than they were to questions about either Alignment or Adherence.

As it turned out, Herman's finding of two distinct aspects, Alignment and Adherence, in a Jewish sample was confirmed for the Sephardic sample; further, the new idea of Affinity for others in the same national group was confirmed in the Sephardic sample. (It was not investigated in earlier research.) Affinity seems to be quite separate from Adherence, but there is some overlap with Alignment. This means that a person's Affinity with others in his national group tells us something about his Alignment with other Sephardim, with regard to beliefs and feelings of separateness from non-Jews; but it tells us very little about the practices characteristic of his daily life as a Sephardi. His Sephardic Identity can be measured much more fully using all three scales than with any two scales, and certainly better than with only one aspect being considered.

Diversity

Sephardic diversity will be presented under two headings, demographic and attitudinal. It must be kept in mind that the numerical data apply only to the 703 respondents whose data were analyzed.

Demographic Diversity

To describe the diversity in demographic characteristics amongst the Sephardim responding to the questionnaire, five tables have been prepared based on the data presented in greater detail in my dissertation (Mizrahi, 1977). Among other things, the demographic results show wide ranges in land of origin, time of immigration, and language diversity. With regard to language, 79% of the respondents speak primarily English at home, and 7% speak primarily French. Interestingly, the majority of participants

(61%) speak a second language in their homes. The high incidence of English as primary language suggests relatively high acculturation, but the high incidence of other languages at home suggests that neither dramatic acculturation nor assimilation can be claimed. Other languages cited by participants are: Arabic, French, Greek, Hebrew, Ladino, Spanish and Turkish.

In Table 1 (page 34) are shown, for each of the eight national groups, the number participating in this study, their average age, and the percent male and female. Also in Table 1, you will find the initials for the national groups used in other tables.

In Table 2 (page 35) are percent values showing the arrival time, using generation as an index, for the national groups; for example, for All respondents, 36% are first-generation arrivals, while for Egyptians (EG), 74% are first-generation arrivals. For the Greeks, 59% reported that their parents were the first generation to arrive.

Of those responding to the survey, Table 3 (page 36) shows that more than 50% have education beyond high school graduation. From Table 5 (page 38), one may see a comparison of socioeconomic status and education for the different national groups.

Finally, the self-reported income and occupation, interpreted as socioeconomic level, is given in Table 4 (page 37). Seventy-four percent of Sephardim reporting for occupation and income are in the top two socioeconomic levels (Hamburger scale, 1958). Because of this study's heavy concentration at the upper socioeconomic levels, statistically valid distinctions at the lower levels could not be made. There still remains much to be learned about the views of non-professional or low-income Sephardim, though they may be among those not reporting for occupation or income and thus socioeconomic status (SES) in this study.

Table 1

Age and Sex of Respondents, by National Group

N	All	BU	EG	GR	IR	MO	SY	TU	EA
		34	46	135	66	50	131	213	28

Means and Standard Deviations for Age of Respondents

	All	BU	EG	GR	IR	MO	SY	TU	EA
M		31.65	44.72	55.04	47.32	41.18	40.94	53.27	61.18
SD		12.85	15.20	13.89	14.22	13.82	13.58	13.97	15.19

Percentages for Sex of Respondents

	All	BU	EG	GR	IR	MO	SY	TU	EA
Female	69	59	67	70	67	70	66	74	54
Male	31	41	33	30	33	30	34	26	46

Note: In this and subsequent tables, the two-letter designations for national groups are as follows: BU, Bukharan; EG, Egyptian; GR, Greek; IR, Iraqi; MO, Moroccan; SY, Syrian; TU, Turkish; and EA, Early American. Unless specifically noted, the N is as shown above.

34

Table 2

Percent of Forebears' Arrival in U.S., by First Generation, by National Group

Generation	All	BU	EG	GR	IR	MO	SY	TU	EA
Own	36	71	74	29	79	80	21	18	–
Parents	45	29	24	59	20	16	38	67	–
Grandparents	14	–	02	12	01	04	36	14	–
Great-grandparents	01	–	–	–	–	–	05	01	–
Before 1840	04	–	–	–	–	–	–	–	100

35

Table 3

Percent of Respondents at Indicated Educational Levels by National Group

Group	N	Less than H.S.	H.S. Grad.	Bus. School Grad.	2-yr. Coll. Deg.	4-yr. Coll. Deg.	Master's Degree	Terminal Prof. Deg.	Academia
Bukharan	34	06	74	03	06	11	-	-	-
Egyptian	46	04	20	04	15	37	09	07	04
Greek	135	14	38	02	07	15	13	07	04
Iraqi	66	02	23	03	15	17	13	27	-
Moroccan	50	04	28	06	18	14	14	06	10
Syrian	131	05	37	03	10	22	06	15	02
Turkish	213	12	40	03	11	14	11	06	03
Early American	28	-	18	-	11	32	07	29	04
All		08	36	03	11	18	10	11	03

Terminal professional degree: e.g., M.D., J.D., LLB, MBA, MSW, MPH.

Academia: Rabbis, Professors at Ph.D. level, nonspecific response of "academia."

36

Table 4

Percent of Persons in Each of Seven Levels of
Socioeconomic Status* by National Group

		Level						
Group	N	1	2	3	4	5	6	7
All	470	40	34	14	08	03	01	-
Bukharan	19	-	53	37	05	05	-	-
Egyptian	29	52	34	10	03	-	-	-
Greek	99	28	43	15	11	01	01	-
Iraqi	49	49	35	12	02	02	-	-
Moroccan	36	42	25	11	17	03	03	-
Syrian	90	57	31	08	08	01	-	-
Turkish	135	30	33	18	10	08	01	-
Early American	13	100	-	-	-	-	-	-

*See Appendix K (Mizrahi, 1987) for the Complete
Hamburger Occupational Scale for Rating Socioeconomic Status. Following are highly abbreviated
notes on Hamburger's seven levels of socioeconomic
status. Hamburger's 1958 money values for income
from own business are updated (1981) as noted below.

Level 1: Postgraduate professionals and very
high value business, producing income of $50,000 or
more.
Level 2: Master degree professionals, own
businesses producing income of $20,000-$50,000.
Level 3: Some professionals requiring bachelors
degree or less, own businesses producing income of
less than $20,000.
Level 4: Semi-professionals.
Level 5: Clerical.
Level 6: Semi-skilled to low-skilled factory or
service occupations.
Level 7: Heavy laborer not regular or stable,
service.

37

Table 5

Rank Orderings for SES and Education,
by Nationlal Group

	Rank Orderings		
National Group	a SES	b Education	% with 4 years College or more
Early American	1	1	62
Syrian	2	4	45
Egyptian	3	2	57
Iraqi	4	2	57
Greek	5	6	43
Moroccan	6	5	44
Turkish	7	7	34
Bukaran	8	8	11

a
  Rank based on the average SES

b
  Rank based on the sum of 4-year college or higher.

Table 6

Percent of Respondents to "Which Groups of Jews Do You Think of as Sephardic?" in Four Categories, by National Group

Group	N	1. Spanish theme	2. Customs and Liturgy	3. Non-Explicit	4. Other Potpourri	No Response
All	659	30	50	09	11	06
Bukharan	25	04	76	16	04	26
Egyptian	42	05	83	07	05	08
Greek	128	43	39	09	09	05
Iraqi	61	13	77	03	07	07
Moroccan	44	20	52	12	16	12
Syrian	121	10	63	17	10	07
Turkish	211	46	32	06	16	01
Early American	27	59	33	–	08	03

Though indications are that American Sephardim are accurately represented in this study as heavily concentrated in the upper socioeconomic levels, conclusions about the completeness of the SES findings cannot be made until questions about sampling are answered. Dr. Solomon Gaon observed (personal communication, 1981) that social standing in the Sephardic community for some Sephardic families is not related to occupation or income, but rather to their long history of social and community prominence in their "old world" country of origin, which is generally known and recognized within the Sephardic community. More information of this kind is discussed in my dissertation, but it is too much to present here.

Participants in this research suggest the breathtaking diversity of American Sephardim. They come from eight different Sephardic national subgroups and from all four of the major strains among American Sephardim referred to on page 3 of this summary: descendants of the "Founding Fathers" of American Jewry; the second and third generation of turn-of-the-century immigrants; a pre- and post-World War II influx; and post-Suez (1956) tide.

Diversity in Attitudes

General Summary

Participants reported significant diversity on the three measures of Sephardic Identity. There was more diversity on the basis of Adherence to the cultural characteristics than on Alignment with other Sephardim. The Syrians were significantly higher in the degree of importance they placed on Adherence; they were followed, in order of attributed importance, by the Egyptians, Greeks and Moroccans. In contrast to the Syrians, the Bukharans and Iraqis were significantly less adherent to the validated cultural characteristics of Sephardim.

Groups of differing national origin did not differ on Alignment, except for the Early Americans, who reported less than the other national groups.

On the Affinity measures, seven of the eight national groups expressed significantly more affinity for their own group than for Sephardim in general. The exception was the Moroccans, for which no reason can be advanced at this time as no relevant data exist. After their own group, Sephardim felt Affinity for American Sephardim, then to American Ashkenazim, then to American Gentiles. The range for all groups is between "very close" and "somewhat close"; even so, these results support the contention that Sephardim represent a set of minorities within a minority.

The Greek and Turkish national groups were well above average on all three measures: Alignment, Adherence, and Affinity. They were also the groups from which most of the respondents came (see Table 1, above). In contrast, the Iraqis were relatively low on all three measures.

From comparisons of attitudes with demographic data, I found that degree of Adherence and Alignment were negatively related to time since forebears' arrival, to amount of education, to use of no language other than English, and to being divorced. Stated the other way around, greater Alignment and Adherence to Sephardic principals and practices would be expected in those who are more recent arrivals, who have less formal education, who use languages(s) other than English at home, and who are not divorced. Remember that the national group to which one belongs may be an indicator of Adherence, and perhaps of Affinity, but not of Alignment.

In Further Detail

When I compared the responses of the eight national groups on the three measures of Sephardic Identity, I found more evidence that the aspects of Alignment, Adherence and Affinity are distinctly different. With regard to Alignment, the Early Americans reported the lowest value (-.66), while the other seven were indistinguishable from each other. The numerical range of group means, as computed, is from approximately -2.00 to +2.00, with an average of 0. Most of the Sephardim in the study have about the same level of Alignment, but the probability that the Early American response is due only to chance is less than 5%; in other words, a statistician would advise us to believe it with great confidence.

With regard to Adherence, six of the groups form a central cluster, with Syrians at one extreme (high Adherence) and Early Americans at the other (low Adherence). The scientific basis of this separation of the set of eight national groups into clusters is very logical. We need to show which groups do not share the same opinions, but at the same time take account of any differences of opinion among members of the same group. If there are large differences within groups, it means the nation-orientation is not consistent with regard to that aspect, and that it would be difficult to tell members of one group from those of another group using only their responses to the questionnaire. So we compare the variations within the groups with the differences between the groups' averages: a lot of difference between group averages with little variation within the groups tells us that the probability that the difference is real is quite high.

With regard to Affinity for Sephardim in general, there is little differentiation among the national groups; although the Early American group is again separate, with lower Affinity, the difference is not statistically supportable, so we should not give much credence to this arithmetical result. For the aspect of Affinity for own national group, six again take the middle ground, with the Syrians high and the Early Americans low. For Affinity with Ashkenazim, there is no statistical separation possible among the eight groups. With regard to Affinity for Gentiles, however, the Early Americans are at the top, with Greek, Iraqi, Turkish and Moroccan in the middle cluster and Egyptian, Syrian and Bukharan reporting lower values on this aspect of Affinity.

It is important to note that the overall averages of the Affinity scale were as follows (on a 1-5 scale):

Own national group	3.86
Sephardim in general	3.57
Ashkenazim	3.08
Gentiles	2.34

This general finding is consistent with my belief that nation-oriented Sephardim can be considered as minorities (national groups within the Sephardic community) within a minority (within Jewry, more affinity for Sephardim than for Ashkenazim) within a minority (more affinity for Sephardim than for Gentiles, and more for Ashkenazim than for Gentiles). The Moroccans are the only national group who did not have more Affinity for their own group than for Sephardim in general; this outcome is interesting, but further exploration would require extensive interviews, and thus speculation here is inappropriate.

Some Speculations

It is tempting to make quick guesses about the emergence (or non-emergence) of differences amongst the national groups, but that desire is to be resisted. Further research can answer well-formed questions leading to the collection of additional information. Nevertheless, on the basis of our study and in the spirit of conservatism, we make the following suggestions, in the hope of stimulating serious further consideration of the complex issues involved.

The Greek-Turkish, Judeo-Spanish speaking Sephardim scored among the highest of the eight subgroups. They were well above the mean on the three criteria for Sephardic Identity. For example, Greeks were third highest on Adherence to typical customs and beliefs, on Affinity for Sephardim in General, and second highest on Affinity for own National subgroup. The Turkish were third highest on Alignment with other Sephardim and on Affinity for own subgroup and second highest on Affinity for Sephardim in General. One possible explanation for the strong Sephardic Identity of the Greek-Turkish group derives from their history. They are those Sephardim who at the time of the Spanish Inquisition were willing to suffer a great deal because of their refusal to convert to Catholicism or even to pretend conversion. They were the Sephardim "... who never changed their faith [not] because they were 'not sophisticated enough to be conversos.' They remained Jews and suffered the torment of expulsion and settlement in their new found homes because they believed theirs was the true faith..." (Benardete, June 1971, p. 25). Thus, Sephardism and the maintenance of their customs have been of extreme importance to the Judeo-Spanish Greek-Turkish Sephardim for the last several hundred years. This still appears to be the case. Another expression of the salience of Sephardism for the Greek-Turkish subgroups perhaps can be found in their extraordinarily strong response to the mailed questionnaire used as data collection in the present study. The Greek-Turkish subgroups together constituted 49% of the total sample of 703 Sephardic respondents, Turkish, 212, and Greek, 135.

The Syrian subgroup reported the strongest adherence to the typically Sephardic customs and values (Adherence), and they also had the most affinity for their own subgroup (Affinity) of the eight subgroups in the study. They were the second highest in socioeconomic status of the eight subgroups. The Early Americans are highest. Eighty-eight percent of the Syrians are in the two highest levels--57% in Level 1 and 31% in Level 2 (Mizrahi, 1987, Tables 6, 9, and 29a). The Syrian immigration pattern is not uniform. Many poor Syrians arrived at the turn of the century, of whom many--like other Sephardim, waves of Ashkenazim, and other poor immigrants of that era--have since risen to the middle and upper-middle classes. Middle and upper-class Syrian Sephardim with entrepreneurial, banking, and professional orientations arrived during the World War II era--with other similarly, previously well established Sephardim from Iran, Iraq, Egypt, and Rhodesia.

One explanation for the Syrian results--strong Adherence to the typically Sephardic customs and values and strong Affinity for their own Syrian subgroup combined with high socioeconomic status and an entrepreneurial orientation--is offered by Sutton (personal communication, May 1986). Aleppo is an ancient city geographically isolated in the extreme northern part of Syria, at a key point on the main caravan trade route across Syria to Baghdad. Aleppo Syrians are overwhelmingly represented in the Syrian sample in the present study (Mizrahi, 1987, Appendix I). Aleppans are characterized as cohesive, religious, and with a particularly strong business and entrepreneurial orientation, in contrast to Damascans, a much smaller group (relatively) from the cosmopolitan centrally located capital of Syria.

In contrast to the Turkish, Greeks, and Syrians, the Bukharans and Iraqis scored relatively low on the measures of Sephardic Identity. The reader is reminded that "relatively low scores" means that subgroup results are presented in ranked order comparing subgroups. Low score means "low" compared with other subgroups in the study. It could still be within a high range. The Bukharans were second lowest on Adherence to the typical customs and beliefs. Perhaps they adhered less strongly to the typical Sephardic characteristics because they were more influenced by Russian than Mediterranean culture, since Bukhara was ceded

45

to Russia in 1868. Also, most Bukharan respondents in the present study recently immigrated to the United States from Israel (Mizrahi, 1987, Appendix I) and thus may have been influenced by the Israeli culture. It is interesting to note that despite their relatively low score on Adherence to the typically Sephardic customs, the Bukharans are second highest on reporting feelings of alignment with other Sephardim regardless of geographical location or time in history (Alignment) and are in the middle on reporting feelings of Affinity for Sephardim in General (ASG). Thus, the Bukharans appear to feel Sephardic in that they feel strong bonds with other Sephardim, though they do not endorse the characteristics considered typical of the group. This disparity between their responses on Adherence contrasted with Alignment and Affinity serves to emphasize the often made point in this and other studies that ethnic identity is multi-dimensional. Individuals may feel a bond to the group though they may not fully endorse the customs considered typical of the group, and vice versa.

The Iraqis ranked relatively low on the measures of Sephardic Identity. They were second lowest on Alignment with other Sephardim and on Affinity for Sephardim in General, and they were third lowest on Adherence to the typical customs and beliefs, and on Affinity for Sephardim of their own national group. One speculation for their relatively weak feelings of Sephardic Identity might be that they hold themselves apart because of great pride in their Iraqi heritage. The Iraqis, unlike the Spanish Sephardic Jews, did not mix with other groups (see page 7). However, these feelings of separateness would not explain why they also felt relatively less Affinity for their own national subgroup than did the other subgroups in the study.

The Early American subgroup answered differently from the other subgroups in the study on nearly all measures of the Sephardic Identity Survey. Of all eight subgroups in the study, the Early Americans had the least Alignment with other Sephardim, the least Adherence to the typically Sephardic customs, the least Affinity for Sephardim in General, and the least Affinity for even their own subgroup (Mizrahi, 1987, Tables Q-2 and Q-3). They constitute the highest socioeconomic group in the study. There are two possible speculations that could explain the Early American subgroup findings. The first is length of time in America; the Early Americans are descended from Sephardim who came to America as early as the 1600s--long before any other Jewish group, Sephardic or Ashkenaze. The second is the difference in cultural influences impinging on their ancestors following the days of the Spanish Inquisition. The Early American Sephardic subgroup consists of Sephardim descended from Spanish Jews who, after 1492, went north to western Europe and Holland before coming to America beginning in the 1600s. The Early American Sephardic subgroup differs from other subgroups in the study who might have also descended from Inquisition day Spanish Jews in that upon leaving Spain, the other subgroups went east to the Ottoman empire and elsewhere, with most of their progeny not arriving in America until the twentieth century. Thus, the Early American subgroup has been the most deeply influenced by western European culture, as opposed to Mediterranean, of all the Sephardic subgroups. This influence existed in unbroken succession from the days immediately following the Inquisition on through the seventeenth century and beyond, when ancestors of the Early American subgroup first settled in European-influenced America.

The foregoing comments underline the diversity between subgroups and have implications not only for the study and understanding of Sephardic Identity but for the study and understanding of other ethnic groups as well. The present study demonstrates that a series of different yet compatible allegiances and identities coexist simultaneously with a strong central Sephardic Identity. Further discussions of the idiosyncracies of the expression of each subgroup's Sephardic identity are beyond the scope of this study. However, they remain an important area for future research. (See the following tables, with page references in the dissertation, for

47

amplification of the above discussion: Table Q-1, p. 492; Table 28, p. 243; Tables Q-2-3, pp. 493-494; Table 31, p. 285.)

Cohesiveness

Four kinds of evidence support the idea of cohesiveness within the Sephardic community. They are:

• results on four questionnaire items indicate cohesiveness and group pride;

• consensus by experts and 703 community members on Sephardic cultural characteristics;

• high rate of response among volunteers;

• high rate of request for summaries.

Four Items Indicate Cohesiveness and Group Pride

Four items were placed in the questionnaire to assess Cohesiveness. They are presented below, with the response mean, on a five-point scale (5 implies greatest agreement).

46.	I feel very Sephardic.	4.20
33c.	Feels pride in Sephardic traditions and history.	4.17
22.	Has inordinate pride in being Sephardic.	4.08
62.	As a Sephardi, feels connected to a group of people with a history of social and cultural prominence in their old world countries of origin.	4.01

The strong endorsement of these items suggests that belonging to the Sephardic group carries for respondents a kind of "magical feeling." One possible explanation for this result is that Iberian Sephardic Jews had a unique experience because their intellectual, social and cultural prominence was accepted and respected during the Golden Age in their own communities and also by the surrounding civilized world, which no other group of Jews had to this extent. Papo, in Sephardim in Twentieth Century America (1986) describes life on the Iberian Peninsula for Sephardic Jews before their expulsion in 1492. Sephardim were not shut off in shtetls but interacted with the larger community in all aspects of their lives. They benefitted from this interaction. Papo writes:

> Medieval Spain--the Golden Age of the Jewish spirit--produced a wondrously rich tapestry of achievement. There were Talmudic scholars ... poets ... scientists ... mathematicians, physicians, cartographers, astronomers ... outstanding religious jurists ... Maimonides, the greatest expounder of Halakhic Judaism, writing The Guide to the Perplexed, to counteract the challenges posed to Judaism by Greek philosophy ... Jewish scholars, by virtue of their knowledge of Hebrew and Arabic as well as Spanish, had access to Greek and even Hindu writings, these writings became available to Jewish scholars living in Christian countries, and their translation from Hebrew to Latin made these writings available to Christian academia ... (1986, p. 5)

After 1492, some members in some groups were able to maintain this advantage. For others, perhaps the "magical feeling" can be explained by pride in traditions that extend back to the earliest known history of mankind.

Sephardic Cultural Characteristics

The author culled sixty-one Sephardic characteristics from an exhaustive computer search of the literature in the field of Sephardic studies, from pilot respondents and from experts in the field of Sephardic studies. She then submitted the sixty-one characteristics to a panel of six experts in the field of Sephardic studies for their consensual validation of whether or not these characteristics were typical of the Sephardic culture. Details of the selection of experts and the rating process appear on page 16 of this summary.

Thirty-one of the original sixty-one characteristics survived the six experts' rating, and these thirty-one characteristics were then transformed into questionnaire items. The 703 Sephardic research participants rated the thirty-one as to degree of importance in their lives.

The list of the six experts with their respective ratings of typicality and the complete list of the original 61 characteristics (with original source) appear in Appendix A of this summary.

Thirty-one of the sixty-one characteristics survived the experts' rating as being at least "typical." They are presented below with corresponding questionnaire number, the original source, followed by the number of its place on the Cultural Characteristic list in Appendix A. Below are two columns of numbers: The first (T) is the experts' average rating of typicality; the second (I) is the 703 participants' average rating of importance. ("5" is very strong, "1" very low.) For example, on Item 1 below, the six experts rated "importance of family" as between "extremely and very typical" (4.17); the 703 participants rated this characteristic as between extremely and very important in their lives (4.49).

Item   Characteristic   T   I

1) *57. My family is very important to me.
        **(Karner) 38   4.17   4.49

---

*Item on questionnaire in Appendix B.
**Original source and place on list of 61 in Appendix B.

2) 40. My sense of honor is of primary importance
to me. (Expert addition) 51   4.67   4.47

3) 37. I have a great deal of pride in myself.
(Benardete) 15   4.00   4.41

4) 79. One must never show disrespect to one's
parents. (Expert addition) 59   4.50   4.34

5) 60. The hospitable entertaining of family,
friends, or neighbors in my own home is
important to me. (Karner, Toledano) 27   4.17   4.32

6) 52. The idea of tradition is important to me.
(Expert addition) 41   4.50   4.29

7) 50. I am very aware of the social manners of
myself and others. (Expert addition) 45   3.00   4.18

8) 63. It is important to teach children Sephardic
traditions and customs. (Karner) 29   4.00   4.15

9) "Pride in being Sephardic" (Benardete) 16
as measured by:

    22. When you meet a Sephardic person, you
want him or her to know you are
Sephardic.   3.50   4.08

10) 62. As a Sephardi, I feel connected to a group
of people with a history of social and
cultural prominence in their old world
countries of origin. (Pilot
respondent) 60   4.17   4.01

11) 19. How important to you is it that children
be named after the parents' parents, even
if living? (Omitted for Iraqi group)
(Angel, 1973; Cardozo) 32   4.67   3.95

12) 73. I have a good business sense. (Pilot
respondent) 58   3.00   3.76

13) "With regard to religion, would have a human-
istic, intellectual, broadminded approach (as
opposed to dogmatism, parochialism and rigid
denominationalism" (Expert addition) 47   4.00
as measured by:
44. (REVERSED ITEM) Judaism should be
seen as a strict and authoritarian consoli-
dation of past learning.   ---   2.52

factored with

45. Judaism should be seen as a cherished
antiquity and passed on to new generations, but an element of controversy is
appropriate.   4.00   3.75

14) "Is interested in own family's Sephardic roots
and genealogy" (Personal experience) 33
as measured by:

20. How interested are you in your family's
Sephardic roots and genealogy? (For
example, do you speak with elders about
it, read books about Sephardim, etc.)   4.67   3.75

factored with

21. When you meet a Sephardic person how

52

interested are you in his or her Sephardic
roots and country of origin?   4.67   3.70

15) 58. Living up to the ways of family elders is
important to me. (Pilot respondent) 44   3.00   3.63

16) 18. (f, d, c and b) Makes Sephardic cooking
an important part of home life (fruit,   4.17   3.61
cheese, nuts or filla pastry for dessert),   3.52
(folded pie crusts stuffed with meat or   3.35
cheese), (rice, cous cous or cracked   3.25
wheat), (vegetables stuffed with rice or
meat). (Omitted for Early American
group) (Angel, 1973; Cardozo;
Toledano) 112

17) 80. When I attend Synagogue, it is important that I attend one with a Sephardic
service. (Cardozo) 36   4.50   3.52

18) 64. With regard to politics and social issues,
I am more likely to be conservative and
traditional rather than liberal. (Pilot
respondent) 54   2.83   3.27

19)   Strict upbringing of children. (Pilot
respondent) 42   3.82
as measured by:
    65. (REVERSED ITEM) Children should not
be raised too strictly   3.25

20) 68. The idea of independence, especially financial independence, should be more emphasized for a boy than a girl. He should
expect to be financially responsible for
himself and/or a family. (Gross) 25, 26   3.17   3.13

21) 26. I frequently visit or am visited by other
          Sephardim as compared with visiting of and
          by non-Sephardim. (Karner) 6   3.17   3.10

22) 53. The man should be felt by others to be
          the boss in the family. (Pilot respond-
          ent) 19,20   3.17   3.09

23) 48. Girls should be raised more strictly
          than boys. (Pilot respondent) 61   4.00   2.86

24) 61. I am a part of a Sephardic community
          where most of my socializing occurs.
          The community is close-knit and mostly
          reserved to people of similar back-
          grounds, which are generally known.
          (Pilot respondent) 43   3.50   2.85

25)   Sephardim are not aggressive group
          organizers. (Expert addition) 50   3.00
          as measured by
     51. (REVERSED ITEM) I work a lot to organ-
          ize for the sake of the Sephardic group.   2.84

26) 27. I give more respect to financial status
          than to advanced academic degrees.
          (Expert addition) 55   3.67   2.81

27)   Frequently attends large Sephardic com-
          munal gatherings. (Gornick) 7   4.00
          as measured by
     59. (REVERSED ITEM) I do not attend
          large Sephardic gatherings.   2.76

28)   Sephardim are innately creative and aes-
          thetic. There is a strong aestheticism

in the culture. (Expert addition) 53   3.67
as measured by
43. (REVERSED ITEM) I am not a crea-
tive nor artistic person.   2.54

29) 56. It is important for Sephardim to marry
Sephardim no matter from which national
group. (Karner) 30   3.67   2.51

30)   Considers self worldly, sophisticated and
versatile by heritage and personality.
(Expert addition) 49   3.67
as measured by
72. (REVERSED ITEM) I am not a worldly
wise person.   2.27

31)   Does not consider work with his hands
beneath his dignity. (Expert addition) 52   3.00
as measured by
(REVERSED ITEM) Working with my
hands is beneath my dignity.   1.77

The content of these 31 items is self-explanatory; clearly a person
endorsing them is probably high on all three of the Sephardic
Identity scales discussed earlier: Alignment, Adherence and
Affinity.   Similar values for national groups have not been
computed, but might be of considerable interest.   The reader is
reminded that the original list of 61 characteristics appears in
Appendix A.

Volunteer Response Rate

Another indication of strong communal feeling was in the
heavy volume of responses to the mailed questionnaire by individuals who were not part of a captive audience. There was no

reward nor approval from a leader for completion of the lengthy, eight-page questionnaire. A responsive chord was struck since 800 responses were returned by mail, 703 of which were usable.

Requests for Summaries

A third index of strong communal feeling can be deduced from the fact that I received nearly 1,000 requests for a summary of the research by the time it was completed; about 700 of these were made when I offered summaries at the time of questionnaire distribution.

Assimilation?

Given the findings reported in the preceding pages, Sephardic Identity has been shown to be statistically supportable as a distinct entity, alive and well (Theory of Sephardic Identity, p. 30). It can be described as traditional, conservative and valuing of the past (Sephardic Cultural Characteristics, page 49). A possible inference is that Sephardic culture might not be highly congruent with either the majority mainstream middle-class American or the American Ashkenaze culture, both of which might be thought of as tending to be more liberal and less traditional. Dramatic assimilation with American culture cannot be claimed even though, paradoxically, Sephardim are notably harmonious with American society in general as indicated by their high socio-economic status. The pattern of parallel cultural lives of American Sephardim is also seen in the language statistics: 79% of the respondents report English as the primary language spoken at home, suggesting acculturation; however, 61% report speaking a second language, suggesting that dramatic acculturation or assimilation cannot be claimed.

There is precedent for Sephardim adapting without

assimilating. Faur (1974), referring to Sephardim of pre-Inquisition days, writes:

Sephardic tradition developed in pluralistic societies ... rather than assimilate ... the Sephardi succeeded in capturing the cultural stimuli of his society and used the key symbols on the non-Jewish world to express the values and ideologies of the Jewish people. (p. 341).

Thus, both because of their special sense of group identity and because American mainstream culture is not congruent with their own, American Sephardim may be expected to continue to value the traditional, family-oriented and conservative characteristics (see page 49 of this summary) typical of Sephardic culture, including the aspects of Alignment, Adherence and Affinity. Accordingly, acculturated American Sephardim may be expected to assimilate less rapidly than some other groups.

Sephardic Personality: A Minority within a Minority

A recognized principle in personality development is that one needs validation by others in order to establish a feeling of self-esteem and belonging (Allport, 1966; Janov, 1960; Lewin, 1948). In part because in America Sephardim are a minority within a minority [only 3 percent of 3 percent (page 1 of this summary)], validation by others may be a social psychological issue. One may ask about the impact on the Sephardi who is aware of both a cluster of positive psychological factors (connection to a group with a distinguished history) and a cluster of negative attitudes ("Outsiders don't understand who I am"); or who for whatever reason experiences the incongruity between Sephardic and American cultures, including the misinformation that leads to the confusion that "Jewish" means only "Ashkenaze." Results from two categories of items raise these Sephardic personality issues. The first category of four items suggests positive psychological factors. The second category of three items suggests negative psychological factors. Both categories invoked some of the strongest feelings on the entire questionnaire, but on opposite ends (4.20 vs. 2.24) of the agreement continuum! For both categories, 5 = strong agreement, while 1 = strong disagreement.)

Category suggesting positive psychological factors:

1. "feel pride in Sephardic traditions and history (#33b)   4.17

2. "has inordinate pride in being Sephardic" (#22)   4.08

3. "As a Sephardi, feels connected to a group of people with a history of social and cultural prominence in their old world countries of origin" (#62)   4.01

4. "I feel very Sephardic" (#46)   4.20

Category suggesting negative psychological factors:

1. "perceives American Gentiles as understanding that there are some differences between Ashkenaze and Sephardic cultures" (#70)   2.24

2. "perceives American Ashkenazim as understanding the role of Sephardim in the development of America" (#74)   2.29

3. "perceives American Ashkenazim as understanding that Sephardim are socially diverse" (#78)   2.86

Issues for future researchers might be which is the stronger influence on personality development, or what is the degree to which an individual Sephardi is able to strike a balance between the positives (connection to a distinguished group) and the negatives (not understood or recognized). One could speculate that there would be a different balance for each individual and for each subgroup.

Another psychological issue involves the extent to which the Sephardi who does not find the emotional or psychological support needed for development from within his family or the Sephardic community can use the outside community as a source of solace, acceptance and affirmation. Seeking options in the outside community may be difficult because the traditional conservative, family-oriented Sephardic culture is not highly congruent with middle-class, mainstream liberal American culture.

Making the transition might be difficult for both Sephardic men and women, but it might be more difficult for women. The role assigned to the man in Sephardic culture is consistent with the "good provider" male sex role expectation in contemporary American culture. However, the role of the woman in Sephardic culture, which is self-actualization through meeting the needs of husband and children, may be less consistent with the female sex role expectation in mainstream, middle-class liberal America. Thus, if the American Sephardic female is able to and wishes to go outside the Sephardic community for affirmation or to seek wider choices, there may be additional conflict for her. She may have to resolve conflicting values and ambivalence towards some of the strong sex role expectations and value system with which she has been imbued since childhood. She could value coming from an old community that was cultured and educated for generations, but reject the limitations inherent in prescribed sex-role behavior. Her cultural sex-role expectation, centered around traditional home, doesn't travel as congruently into middle-class, mainstream liberal American culture as does the Sephardic male's "good provider" sex role expectation.

Validation by others may be a problem for Sephardim, not

only because of divergence from the majority mainstream, middle-class liberal American personality, but also because of the confusion about Sephardic culture. The above results (page 58) suggest that while Sephardim feel pride in their heritage, they also perceive that outsiders don't know what that is. In America, Jews are mistakenly viewed as a homogeneous group, to mean only "Ashkenaze." When one hears "Jewish," one thinks of the Ashkenaze Jews who emigrated from eastern or central Europe, and one thinks in terms of certain values, traditions, time of immigration, tastes in food, and of language--German and its derivative, Yiddish. For those intelligentsia who may be aware of Sephardim, there is often confusion and stereotypic thinking and the incorrect belief that American Sephardim are either the "Grandees" or impoverished recent immigrants. In fact, American Sephardim are extremely diverse, comprising at least four major strains based primarily on differing times and circumstances of immigration (see page 3).

In summary, future researchers in personality may find it useful to study the interrelationship of forces converging on some American Sephardim, not only for the benefit of that group alone, but because American Sephardim provide an excellent example of two well-defined cultures coexisting harmoniously in parallel, but with a potential for dramatic psychological interaction, both between and within individuals.

"Why does this magnificent applied science which
saves work and makes life easier bring us so
little happiness? The simple answer runs:
Because we have not yet learned to make
sensible use of it."
--Albert Einstein, Address
California Institute of Technology
February 1931

5. IMPLICATIONS

Four categories of implications are addressed in this chapter:
definition of Sephardim, revisited; education; counseling
psychology; and further research.

Definition of Sephardim, Revisited

In previous discussion (page 29), it was brought out that
there was an apparent lack of a clear-cut commonly accepted
definition among Sephardim themselves about whether it should
be restricted to direct Iberian ancestry (30%) or should include
possible direct Iberian ancestry but follow Sephardic customs and
liturgy (50%). As with other potential "marking-off by others"
items, this apparent lack of a clear-cut definition among
Sephardim themselves which reflects the lack of agreement among
experts in the field has implications not only for the study of
Sephardic Identity per se, but for correlates of Sephardic Identity
such as self-esteem, self-concept, and sense of belonging. To carry
this research to a successful conclusion, one should develop a
fairly extensive questionnaire dealing primarily with the definition,
using both open-ended and multiple choice formats for the

questions. Great care should be given to the sampling plan in such a study, so that inferences may be based on responses representative of a clearly definable reference group.

Education

In this section, we refer to the clear need for more information about American Sephardim; the results of this study are focused on what educators could use to meet these needs.

Need for Information about Sephardim

The teaching of American history in our country has been perceived as inadequate or distorted because it does not include the contributions of different minority groups. Calls for correct information about American Sephardim have appeared for years in journals, book reviews, interviews, symposium proceedings, and the like. An editorial in Human Behavior (6/76) reports A. D. Lavander (University of Maryland) complaining that "Sephardim are usually neglected by both lay persons and social scientists who study Jews in America." In an article in the Jewish Chronicle (4/18/75) titled "Is Sephardism Alive," Maurice Pitchon speculated that "Maybe the basic problem is that we Sephardim do not understand ourselves what Sephardism is." Although Birmingham's 1971 The Grandees had the distinct value of awakening the public to the contributions of Sephardic Early Americans, it was misleading about and perpetuated misconceptions of the other Sephardic American groups. "His book is plagued with factual inaccuracies and poor historical perspectives," wrote Dr. Marc Angel (6/71, p. 16) in one of four reviews which criticized Birmingham's book, all published by the Foundation for the Advancement of Sephardic Studies and Culture, Inc. S. Zion's review of Birmingham was noted earlier (page 1).

The American Sephardi Foundation has also been active in promoting educational efforts through workshops and study guides (Campeas, 1978).

What Educators Can Use From This Study

The present study provides a portrait of some of the opinions and practices, and details demographic characteristics and cultural characteristics of present day Sephardim on the East Coast of the United States.

American Sephardim are extremely heterogeneous in terms of time and circumstances of immigration, land of origin and attitudes (endorsement of the three Sephardic Identity factors called Alignment, Adherence and Affinity).

In itself, the study as reported is not a training program, nor a syllabus such as Faur's (1974) excellent "Introducing the Materials of Sephardic Culture to Contemporary Jewish Studies." This study contains results from a largely volunteer group of 703 respondents, a fact which educators will note as they draw upon it for inferences about this ethnic group. Most notable among these are

• the special pride in their heritage and strong group feeling despite considerable diversity amongst Sephardim (page 48);

• the dramatic demographic diversity within cohesiveness amongst American Sephardim, linked not just to nation of origin but to time and circumstances of emigration to America which comprises at least four major strains (pages 3 and 32);

• the evidence supporting the contention that nation of origin plays a role in establishing subgroups among the Sephardim, who may be referred to as "minorities within a minority" (page 40);

- the comprehensive listing of 61 Sephardic cultural characteristics with respective ratings for typicalty of Sephardic culture, given consensually by a panel of six experts in the field of Sephardic Studies (Appendix A). The 31 characteristics, from the original list of 61, which survived the experts' ratings for Sephardic typicality. These 31 validated characteristics with the six experts' ratings compared with the 703 participants' ratings of importance in their lives appear on page 49;

- the lack of a clear-cut commonly accepted definition of "Sephardim" by participants in this research as well as by experts in the field, which involves the controversy of direct Iberian descent as a condition (pages 7, 29, 39 and 61);

- further research into the ideational and behavioral criteria of Sephardic Identity as comprised of at least three aspects-- Alignment, Adherence, and Affinity--and the degree to which they are endorsed by Sephardim (pages 30 and 40);

- the importance of the problem of American Sephardic Identity for Sephardim and also because of its parallel to other ethnic groups, whose specific identity is submerged under a broader category. In America, Sephardim comprise only 3% of all Jews, who themselves are less than 3% of the total population. American Sephardic Identity, therefore, is embedded and buried under the general concept of Jewish Identity, which in America generally reflects Ashkenaze traditions and culture. Other groups are often thought of as homogeneous despite their considerable heterogeneity, for example, American Blacks (page 57);

- an extensive review of literature which appears in the dissertation itself (Mizrahi, Chapter 2, 1987). It includes reviews of studies, theories and research related to: Concept of Identity (including Allport and Erikson); Concept of

Reference Group Theory and Ethnic Identity; Previous Research and Studies related to Ethnic Identity (including substantial sections on the several epochs of research devoted to Jewish Identity); and the Sephardic Group in America and elsewhere.

The broad strokes in this summary should be supplemented by inspection and study of the wealth of detail in the dissertation itself (Mizrahi, 1987).

Counseling Psychology

Ethnic Identity is a force in the lives of all clients to some extent. One of the worst things that can be done in counseling is inaccurate stereotyping. This study is a sensitizer for counselors to the impact of cultural forces on personality. Alignment, Adherence, and Affinity can be used as guidelines by counseling psychologists in furthering their understanding that identity is multidimensional, whether for Sephardim or for other groups. Affinity or the lack thereof for one's particular subgroup has implications for self-esteem and self concept for some clients. Ethnic Identity may be an area of struggle for some clients. A client may feel conflict on some dimensions of identity and not on others--for example, the present study showed that an individual Sephardi may have strong affinity for his own national group or for Sephardim in general, but may not necessarily endorse in his daily life those behaviors that are considered typically Sephardic.

There is some evidence that counselors who differ from their clients in culture, race or social class have greater difficulty communicating with their clients and that these differences limit an empathetic and understanding climate (Pedersen, 1978). The extent to which this study contributes to that understanding and empathy is its contribution to professional practice in Counseling

Psychology. This study provides a tool for expanding the counselor's awareness and reducing his ethnocentrism.

Future Research

Methodology

This study was designed with great attention to the objectives, and conducted with careful examination of the results of each step before proceeding to the next. The major steps are summarized in earlier sections of this summary (pages 13-25) and presented in much greater detail in the dissertation itself (Mizrahi, 1987). One should attend to new approaches in assessment, beyond the questionnaire. Field observations should be undertaken to verify the self-reports on which this study is based. Different styles of asking questions should be tried, even the inevitable paper-and-pencil inventory approach, so that probing of the respondent's views may supplant his choice of the "best answer," especially when none of the alternatives may be what he had in mind.

New techniques of data analysis have been developed since this study was conducted; more sophisticated kinds of factor analysis are possible, and one may go directly to the problem of forming groups of persons based on their responses (cluster analysis), instead of having to rely on external identification which may make too much of stereotyping or ostensible group membership. Techniques are available to examine multiple responses from a single respondent, thus allowing greater insight into the individual's dynamics.

Finally, new research should attend to the sampling problem; techniques of telephone interviewing have advanced greatly, and the adaptability of computers to almost everything bodes well for new exciting forms of data collection, where anyone near a computer is accessible to any researcher.

Theory of Sephardic Identity

Numerous implications emerged for future research in Sephardic Identity in addition to those pertaining to Sephardic personality (page 57) and the definition of "Sephardim" (page 61):

(1) Further exploration of the structuring of the three facets of Sephardic Identity and refinement of items might be useful.

(2) Further investigation of intra-subgroup differences would be interesting, since standard deviations showed there was substantial variability within subgroups (Mizrahi, 1987, Tables Q-1 through Q-5). For example, future in-depth exploration of intra-subgroup diversity might relate to direct Spanish ancestry; in the Greek, Syrian, Moroccan and other subgroups, some individuals are of Spanish ancestry while others are not. Direct Iberian ancestry may have implications for Sephardic Identity and sense of belonging. Also, city of origin within a particular old world country of origin may have implications. Are there significant differences between the entrepreneurial Aleppans and the Damascans? Between the Janina Greeks who have always been Greek and the Greek Jews from Salonika who speak Judeo-Spanish? Also, differential time of immigration to America within a particular subgroup may be a significant variable within subgroups, affecting not only Identity itself, but correlates of identity such as self-esteem and sense of belonging. Some subgroups in the study immigrated more uniformly than others; 76% of the Bukharans in the study immigrated since 1960, and 100% of the Early Americans (by definition) had ancestors in America before 1840. However, Greek, Moroccan, Syrian and Turkish respondent immigration spans the century (Mizrahi, 1987, Table 4).

67

(3) Future researchers might try to obtain a larger, preferably randomly sampled population to learn more about the high socioeconomic status reported by respondents in this research-- 74% of those reporting for occupation and income are in the top two SES levels (Hamburger scale, 1958). Though indications are that American Sephardim are accurately represented in the upper socioeconomic levels, conclusions about the completeness of the SES findings cannot be made until questions about sampling are answered. In this study, an enormous, largely successful effort was made to reach as broad and diverse a Sephardic group as possible by using and then going beyond Yeshiva University's comprehensive mailing list. Eventually, questionnaires were distributed to nearly 5,000 east coast American Sephardim! It is possible, but costly and very time-consuming, to reach a larger, thus potentially more representative, sample. The value of a random, representative sample is that one can then make valid inferences to the general population. The extent to which this study succeeds in representativeness is the extent to which inferences can be made.

(4) Future studies on Sephardic Identity should expand the religious behavior component on the Adherence Criterion. In this study, unfortunately, eight questionnaire items pertaining to religiosity had to be deleted, mainly for technical reasons. Two items pertaining to religiosity remained in the questionnaire. Detailed discussion appears in the dissertation itself (Mizrahi, 1987, page 122).

(5) Future Sephardic studies might examine an even larger range of Sephardic national subgroups than the eight in this research. Even that figure missed some, for example, the Bulgarians and the Iranians.

Ethnic Identity Theory

Perhaps Alignment, Adherence and Affinity are relevant

68

for the study of other groups, especially those comprised of subgroups. The present study confirms that Herman's theory of Jewish Identity is very useful as a point of departure for application to the study of American Sephardic Identity.

The dimension of Affinity is an original contribution of this researcher to the context of Ethnic Identity. While it was especially called for in a study of the diverse American Sephardic group, it may or may not be called for in other studies of Ethnic Identity. For example, Polish, Russian or German subgroup membership might be important to individual Ashkenazim. Or subgroup Affinity might be important in a study of American Blacks. Haitians, British West Indians, Spanish-speaking Cubans and Puerto Ricans, Virgin Islanders, and native Africans, as well as American Blacks are frequently thought of homogeneously as "black" despite their considerable heterogeneity. The concept of Affinity warrants much more investigation.

Three Criteria Guide Questionnaire Development

Below in Figure 3 is a simplified framework to give the general reader a sense of the process by which the three criteria were used as a basis for questionnaire item development. A full accounting appears in great detail in the dissertation itself, and educators and researchers are referred to that source. The reader of this monograph is referred to pages 16, 49 and elsewhere for more on development and results pertaining to the Sephardic Cultural Characteristics, which was an enormous research effort in itself, but necessary before I could write Criterion 2 questions. I hope the three-criteria model I devised to measure Sephardic Identity will provide a basis and impetus for refinement and extension of this important area of research.

69

FIG. 3. FRAMEWORK FOR MIZRAHI SEPHARDIC IDENTITY SURVEY: THREE CRITERIA

ALIGNMENT - measures the individual's feelings about relationships as a Sephardi
   a. Marking Off (how self and others differentiate him as a Sephardi)
      1. By Self - how the Sephardi feels different from members of other groups (e.g., q. #31) *
      2. By Others - how the Sephardi perceives others differentiating him (e.g., q. #70)
   b. Alignment (how aligned within the Sephardic group, the Sephardi feels)
      1. Across Space - how close the Sephardi feels to other Sephardim around the world
         (e.g., q. #32)
      2. Across Time - the Sephardi's sense of belonging with Sephardim of the past, present and
         future (e.g., q. #49)

ADHERENCE - measures the importance in his daily life which the individual gives to (adheres to)
characteristics validated by six Sephardic scholars as, "typically Sephardic" (See pages 16, 49, 74 and 75).
The cultural behaviors are organized in five categories:

1. Inter- and intra-family behaviors (e.g., q. #57) *
2. Sex roles (e.g., q. #53)
3. Religiosity (e.g., q. #44 compared with #45)

    4. Self-image (e.g., q. #62)
    5. Financial behavior (e.g., q. #73)

AFFINITY - to comparatively measure closeness to one's own Sephardic national sub-group (e.g. Greek),
with Sephardim in General and with non-Sephardim. The answers to questions 31-35 and 46 were used in
a factor analysis to give this comparative information. For example, closeness is measured for Sephardim in
General in q. #31a; Sephardim of own National Group, q. #31b; Ashkenazim, q. #31c;
Gentiles, q. #31D; and so on for questions 32 through 35.

---

*   Question numbers refer to the Questionnaire, Appendix B, page 89.
The above diagram is just an example of how questions were designed based on the criteria and is not
meant to show the entire questionnaire. Each of the three critera was measured with many more questions
than could fit on this page. Full details appear in the dissertation (1987).

"What we call results are beginnings."
--Emerson, Representative Man; Plato

6. CONCLUSION

What can be concluded from this rigorous empirical study of Sephardic Identity? First, the aspects of identity proposed by Herman from his analysis of Israeli Jews was shown to be applicable to measuring differences in Alignment and Adherence amongst New York-New Jersey area Sephardim. Second, the newly considered aspect of Affinity was shown to be different than those put forth by Herman and also proved much more sensitive to differences arising from different national groups. It appears that differences arising from national origin are slight with regard to Alignment and Adherence, with Adherence showing the greater effect. The salient conclusion from this effort, stated very conservatively, is that Sephardim do indeed form a distinctive group within Jewry, but that except for the Early Americans, national origin seems to be a relatively minor, but frequently statistically significant contributor to differences in identity. Other significant contributors to differences in Sephardic Identity were time of family's immigration to America, amount of education, use of no language other than English, and marital status.

Despite the considerable diversity amongst participants, strong communal feeling and pride was evidenced. One interpretation of the Affinity results argues for a sense of group unity amongst participants since the Affinity measures were close for both national group and Sephardim in general. A rich data base emerged from the characteristics that the author identified and the experts validated which should be refined and augmented by future researchers.

When I began my research in the 1970's, very little had been written about the complexities of the Sephardic American groups. Now, some years later, books and articles have appeared; for example, Joseph Papo's (1987) <u>Sephardim in Twentieth Century America</u> is particularly apt for the times because it calls for unity and gives an overall perspective. Also, books such as Dalven's <u>The Jews of Janina</u> about Greek-speaking Jews, Daniel J. Elazar's <u>The Balkan Jewish Communities: Yugoslavia, Bulgaria, and Turkey,</u> and Dr. M. Kayserling's <u>Christopher Columbus and the Participation of the Jews in the Spanish and Portuguese Discoveries</u> can all be obtained through New York's American Sephardi Federation.

It is clear that there is a great variety of implications of this research, not only for the study of the American Sephardic community, but probably of other ethnic groups, as we work towards a more elegant and refined differentiation of personality and individual characteristics. This study will be of value to the extent that it extends understanding of individual variability, a basic premise in psychology, and furthers understanding of the subtleties and variances within American group life.

Appendix A

Expert Weighting of Cultural Characteristics

Part 1. Experts in Sephardic Studies Who Rated the Characteristics

Part 2. Original 61 Characteristics, Complete Expert Ratings, Original Sources, and Corresponding Questionnaire Item Numbers

73

Part 1.

Experts in Sephardic Studies
Who Rated the Characteristics*

David F. Altabe, Associate Professor, Department of Foreign Languages and Literature, Queensborough Community College; President, American Society of Sephardic Studies

Rachel Dalven, Ph.D., Professor Emeritus of English, Ladycliff College

The Haham, Rabbi Solomon Gaon, Ph.D., Chief Rabbi of the World Sephardi Federation; President of the Union of the Sephardi Congregations of America and Canada; Holder of the Chair of Sephardic Studies at Yeshiva University; and, Holder of the Maybaum Chair in the Rabbinics at Yeshiva University

Joseph Papo, MSW, Past Executive Director, Central Sephardic Jewish Community of America

Rabbi M. Mitchell Serels, Ph.D., Director, Sephardic Community Activities Program, Sephardic Studies Program, Yeshiva University

Henry Toledano, Ph.D., Associate Professor, Director of Jewish Studies, Hofstra University

---

*The particular ratings of the above experts are identified in the following pages only as those of Expert A, Expert B, etc., and are in no special order.

Part 2.

Original 61 Characteristics, Complete Expert Ratings, Original Sources, and Corresponding Questionnaire Item Numbers

Key to Ratings of Sephardic Characteristics*

5. **Extremely typical

4. Very typical

3. Typical

2. Somewhat typical

1. Not typical

-----

*In some instances the following characteristics are not quoted "word for word," but are paraphrased from sources appearing in the bibliography. In some instances the characteristic was meant by the source to apply to a particular Sephardic national subgroup but is included in the following list for evaluation by the expert-consultants or its application to the Sephardic culture in general.

**In the Computer Analysis, the above values were utliized. They were reversed at the time of Expert Rating.

Expert Weighting of Cultural Characteristics with Corresponding Questionnaire Item Number

Characteristic	Expert						Average	Questionnaire Item #
	A	B	C	D	E	F		

1. Celebrates Sabbath by eating   3 4 3 3 n/r 2
   of typical Sephardic foods, i.e.,   = 15/5   3   omitted
   fish first, then meat cooked with
   vegetables, hard-boiled eggs may be served, followed by rice; time for family
   get-together. (Content by Youcha, 1973; Order from personal communication)

   Revisions: The particular foods are not necessarily typical but rather vary
   with each subgroup. (Toledano)

2. Believes in mysticism.   2 3 2 1 4 2
   (Benardete, 1953, p. 75)   = 14/6   2.4   omitted

   Revision: Does not believe in superstition. This overlooks Maimonides and
   the rational tradition of the Spanish-Portuguese era, and it overlooks the
   influence of the Alliance-Israelite whose efforts were aimed at wiping out
   mystical influence. (Altabe)
   Most Sephardim tend towards rationalism. (Toledano)

3. Disapproves of taking charity.   2 4 1 4 2 5
   (Angel, 1973, p. 93)   = 18/6   3   omitted

4. Feels Sephardic rather than   1 1 2 1 1 3
   American or other nationality.   = 9/6   1.5   omitted

   Revisions: Has a negative aspect. Not only do they feel Sephardic, but they
   distinguish themselves by their subgroups. Discrimination between subgroups.
   (Dalven)
   One can feel very Sephardic in terms of his Jewishness, but still feel
   American in terms of his nationality. (Toledano)

5. Knows or has read about Rabbi   n/a 3 1 1 1 1
   Yaakov Hulli's Na'am Lo'ez.   = 7/5   1.4   omitted

   Revisions: This statement would be more applicable to the Judeo-Spanish

76

speaking subgroups thatn to other Sephardim, however, it is still not typical. (Papo)

6. Frequently visits other Sephar-dim at home and is visited at home by other Sephardim. (Karner, 1969)

	A	B	C	D	E	F			
	4	3	3	3	4	2	= 19/6	3.2	26

Revisions: There's a time element here. In the past they were more concerned about who their children married so they often met and entertained at home. Now there are more communal relationships than home relationships. (Dalven)

7. Frequently attends large Sephardic communal gatherings (Gornick, 1975)

	A	B	C	D	E	F			
	3	5	3	4	4	5	= 24/6	4	59

Revisions: Communal parties rather than gatherings. (Papo)

8. Honors the dead by participa-ting in a group gathering at the anniversary of the death, at which time there may be a reading of the Bible, celebration honoring the deceased, stories told, coffee and perhaps food served, with many in attend-ance. (Benardete, 1953, pp. 117-118)

	A	B	C	D	E	F			
	5	3	3	2	4	4	= 21/6	3.5	omitted

Revisions: Traditionally, they all go at the time of the death of one from the community, but in modern times, fewer attend. Must consider the changing times, especially in New York. (Dalven)
There are even specific celebrations, e.g., Hilula, in Morocco and in Israel, which celebrates the anniversary of the death of certain Jewish saints. (Toledano)

9. Accepts that the man is the head of the family, i.e., the ultimate decision maker, but the woman does in fact exert power to the extent that she successfully fulfills the needs of her husband and children. (Personal communication)

	A	B	C	D	E	F			
	2	3	3	5	4	3	= 20/6	3.3	25

Revisions: Perhaps it's a covert matriarchy. (Altabe)

The Sephardic women that I know are extremely strong in the household but the manifestation of her power is related to the economic contribution of the male--depending on the strength of the man as a provider. She gives him authority if he is a good provider. The Sephardic culture is a subtle matriarchal society. If a woman is successful through her cooking and then the husband is awed by this, and she has a strong influence in the community and in the household. The oppressive element of the matriarchy is so strong that it can cause the man to feel intimidated and thus take a recessive position so far as his "fatherhood" is concerned. (Dalven)

The position of the man in the family is the head of the family in the Sephardic culture. This is not necessarily the result of an attitude of dominance on the part of the husband, but rather it is one of respect and reverence shown to the man by the rest of the family including the wife. (Toledano)

10. Speaks language other than 5 1 1 1 4 4
English at home, e.g., Judeo-   = 16/6   2.7   omitted
Spanish, Judeo-Greek, Judeo-
Arabic, French, Spanish, etc. (Karner, 1969)

Omitted from analysis since typical but with numerous qualifications.

11. Feels kinship when meets other 4 4 3 4 4 4
Sephardi. (Angel, 1973, p. 127)   = 23/6   3.8   omitted

Revisions: Yes, however other considerations strengthen or weaken the kinship, e.g., level of education, language and social class are very strong determinants. (Dalven)

When meets others from same national subgroup there is a feeling stronger than kinship. (Toledano)

Omitted: Explored elsewhere on questionnaire.

12. Makes Sephardic cooking a 5 5 3 2 4 5
major aspect of home life; the   = 23/6   3.8   18a-f
Sephardic foods emphasized
might be meat (often lamb) cooked with vegetables or beans, lamb cooked with

	Expert						Average	Questionnaire Item #
Characteristic	A	B	C	D	E	F		

eggplant, pastries may be cooked with "filla," rice rather than potatoes (often eaten after the meat or fish), arak as the liquor, coffee may be Turkish rather than American or French. (Angel, 1973, p. 125; Cardozo, 1965/66)

Revisions: Yes, they all use dill for example inthe foods,and everyone knows "filla." All the Sephardim eat grape leaves and burekia (with meat, cheese or spinach). These dishes are well known, staples if you will. (Dalven)

Sephardic foods are a major aspect of home life. However, what foods served will depend on the subgroup. For example, Moroccan foods would be cous cous and skhina (eggs, potatoes, rice and meat). Skhina is equivalent to Ashkenaze chulat. (Toledano)

13. Believes that femininity is demonstrated by competence in home care areas. (Sephardic World, Vol. I, 1972)

	A	B	C	D	E	F	Average	Item #
13.	2	3	3	4	4	5	3.5	omitted

= 21/6

Revisions: The Sephardim are very aesthetic and they like to marry nice looking women. The word "feminine" has to do with personal attractiveness. A Sephardic male's rating of a woman as his wife depends on her ability and desire to take care of the house and her husband and family. Traditionally, it was unheard of if the man helped in the household; and, it can be added that if he did try to get into "her" area, she might be annoyed. (Dalven)

14. Believes that masculinity is demonstrated by early economic independence. (Sephardic World, Vol. I, 1972)

	A	B	C	D	E	F	Average	Item #
14.	1	2	3	2	4	5	2.8	omitted

= 17/6

15. Has inordinate pride in self. Benardete, 1953, p. 146)

	A	B	C	D	E	F	Average	Item #
15.	4	5	3	5	3	4	4	37

= 24/6

Revisions: This characteristic should be split by sex. If a man, he will have inordinate pride in himself. The man is trained to feel the superior one. The woman's job is to love, honor and obey the man. The man has been trained to have more pride. (Dalven)

Characteristic	Expert						Average	Questionnaire Item #
	A	B	C	D	E	F		
16. Has inordinate pride in being Sephardic. (Benardete, 1953, p. 146)	4	3	1 = 21/6	4	4	5	3.5	22,23,2
17. If a woman, believes that men have more importance in the family unit. (Male child is king,	2	3	2 = 19/6	4	3	5	3.2	omitted

served by sisters; decisions in family brought to eldest brother; men served coffee first beginning with the eldest downward, and then women beginning with the eldest and downward. (Youcha, 1973)

Revisions: Omit "decisions brought to eldest brother." The mother in the family would not do this. (Altabe)

Sephardic women are trained to be subordinate to their men. They are trained to serve them. If the first child is male, he is given authority as a second father and is called Behor. Very often this oldest son makes the decisions about whom his sisters should marry. The tradition is that the woman must be supported by the man and in return she willingly gives herself completely to caring for him, the family and the house. In the past, she was like a chattel and had no powers of any kind. The Katubah, the marriage contract was interpreted as the "declaration of independence" for a woman. (Dalven)

Omitted: other male dominance items on list.

Characteristic	Expert						Average	Questionnaire Item #
18. If a man, believes that men have more importance in the family unit. (Male child is	3	3	2 = 18/6	2	3	5	3	omitted

king, served by sisters; decisions in family brought to eldest brother; men served coffee first beginning with eldest and downward, and then women beginning with eldest and downward. (Youcha, 1973)

Revisions: Mainly it is important to give the impression to outsiders that she is not dominant and her husband is. (Altabe)

Characteristic	Expert						Average	Questionnaire Item #
19. If a woman, believes in the following statements: a. The man is the overt boss in the family.	5	2	2 = 19/6	2	3	5	3.2	53,54

Characteristic	Expert						Average	Questionnaire Item #
	A	B	C	D	E	F		
b. All men should be tough and valiant.	1	2	2	2	3	5		
c. A man is a man as long as he can prove it. (omitted by two experts)	n/a	2	2	2	3	5		
d. The place for women is in in the home.	3	2	2	2	3	5		
			= 17/6				2.8	
e. Men are more intelligent than women. (Extended from Youcha source) (Fernandiz-Marina scale on male dominance)	1	2	2	2	3	1		

Revisions: The woman believes the man's job and her children are more important than a job of her own.

The woman doesn't believe generally that the Sephardic man is more intelligent; the woman gives him authority simply because he's male. The Sephardic woman has a keen intelligence as well. The man is the overt boss. She would like the man to be intelligent and modern rather than tough. (Dalven)

20. If a man, belives in the following statements:

Characteristic	Expert						Average	Questionnaire Item #
a. The man is the overt boss in the family.	5	2	2	2	3	5		
			= 19/6				3.2	53,54
b. All men should be tough and valiant.	3	2	2	2	3	5		
c. A man is a man as long as he can prove it. (omitted by two experts)	n/a	2	2	2	3	5		
d. The place for women is in the home.	5	2	2	2	3	5		
			= 19/6				3.2	
e. Men are more intelligent than women (extended from Youcha source) (Fernandiz-Marina scale on male dominance)	1	2	2	2	3	5		

21. If a man, believes that the social position of the wife is in direct proportion to the social position of the husband. (Benardete, 1953)

	4	3	4	4	2	5		
			= 22/6				3.7	omitted

	Expert						Aver-age	Ques-tion-naire
Characteristic	A	B	C	D	E	F	age	Item #

Revisions: He wants his wife to have the same social position he has once he marries her. (Dalven)

22. If a woman, believes that the social position of the wife is in direct proportion to the social position of the husband. (Benardete, 1953)
    4 3 4 5 3 5 = 24/6   4   omitted

23. Believes in more exposure to education for boys than for girls. (Karner, 1969)
    2 1 4 4 3 5 = 19/6   3.2   omitted

Revisions: It depends on the particular subgroup. (Toledano)

Omitted: See Dalven Addition #2.

24. Has as strong emotional attach-ment to land of family origin (e.g., Spain, Greece, Syria, Balkan countries, Middle-East, Turkey, etc.) (Angel, 1973)
    4 4 1 1 3 2 = 15/6   2.5   omitted

25. If a man, belives that children of different sexes should be reared differently; for boys, an emphasis on learning of money related matters; for girls, emphasis on home care aspects. (Gross, 1966)
    2 3 2 4 3 5 = 19/6   3.2   68

Revisions: The man always hopes that his son will enter the same business or profession. (Dalven)
May be very typical of one Sephardic subgroup and very non-typical of other subgroups. (Toledano)

26. If a woman, believes that chil-dren of different sexes should be reared differently; for boys, an emphasis on learning of money related matters; for girls, emphasis on home care aspects. (Gross, 1966)
    2 3 2 4 3 5 = 19/6   3.2   68

	Expert						Aver-age	Ques-tion-naire
Characteristic	A	B	C	D	E	F		Item #

Revisions: The boy is given much greater freedom in being reared. Many more restrictions on the girls. (Dalven)

27. Feels that hospitality is impor- 5 5 3 5 3 4
tant. (Karner, 1969) (Hospi- = 25/6   4.2   60
tality is defined as generous or
cordial entertaining of immediate family, extended family, friends and/or neighbors.

Revisions: Hospitality is important because family is extremely important. (Dalven)
Feelings of hospitality are not ones of obligation. They stem out of enjoy-
ment. (Toledano)

28. If a man, engages in trade as 4 1 4 n/a 3 3
an occupation. (Karner, 1969) = 15/5   3   omitted

Revisions: This characteristic is outdated. Males are now more interested
in the professions and in academia. (Altabe)
Modern times are different. This was more true in past--of the older generation. (Dalven)
Commerce should be added to trade. (Toledano)

29. Feels it is important to teach 5 2 3 4 5 5
children Sephardic traditions. = 24/6   4   63
(Karner, 1969)

Revisions: Omit "teach" and replace with "indoctrinate." It was a matter of
survival for the parents. (Dalven)

30. Believes strongly in the dictum 3 2 5 2 5 5
that one's marriage partner = 22/6   3.7   55,56
should be from within the
Sephardic community. (Karner, 1969)

Revisions: Preferably within the subgroup but also strongly within the
Sephardic community.

Characteristic	A	B	C	D	E	F	Average	Questionnaire Item #
31. Practices Sephardic liturgy in private life. (Personal communication)	3	3	1	1 = 18/6	5	5	3	omitted

Revisions: If religious. (Toledano)

Characteristic	A	B	C	D	E	F	Average	Questionnaire Item #
32. Believes in naming children according to a special system.	3	5	5	5 = 28/6	5	5	4.7	19

(First born son after the father's father, second son after the mother's father, third son after brother or relative of father, fourth son after brother or relative of mother; for girls, the same is true, i.e., first daughter after father's mother, etc.) (Angel, 1973, p. 125; Cardozo, 1965/66)

Characteristic	A	B	C	D	E	F	Average	Questionnaire Item #
33. Has a "Sephardic-genealogical consciousness."	5	5	4	5 = 28/6	4	5	4.7	20,21

("Sephardic-genealogical consciousness" defined as an interest in and an awareness of the Sephardic roots of self and others. (Personal experience)

Characteristic	A	B	C	D	E	F	Average	Questionnaire Item #
34. Practices folklore surrounding the wedding ceremony; months in assembling the trousseau,	3	4	2	1 = 11/5	n/a	1	2.2	omitted

special days for special customs including the bride going to the bathhouse with other women where she's cleansed and she shares a repast with other women. (Patai, 1953)

Revisions: In the past it was extremely typical, but now it isn't. (Dalven. It was extremely, at least in some subgroups like the Yeminites in Morocco, until very recently. But this is no longer practiced. (Toledano)

Characteristic	A	B	C	D	E	F	Average	Questionnaire Item #
35. Believes in observance of Capora; a special preparation of chicken before Yom Kippur. (Personal communication)	4	1	2	1 = 9/5	n/a	1	1.8	omitted

Revisions: Word is "Kapporat." (Dalven) (Toledano)

	Expert						Aver-	Ques-tion-naire
Characteristic	A	B	C	D	E	F	age	Item #

Characteristic	A	B	C	D	E	F	Average	Item #
36. Attends Synagogue with Sephardic liturgy. Hazan, the reader leads the singing with congregational participation, chanting of whole congregation; music repetitive and joyous. (Cardozo, 1965/66, pp. 11-39)	5	3	5 = 27/6	4	5	5	4.5	80
37. Views Sephardic customs as major guiding social force. (Karner)	4	2	4 = 20/6	1	4	5	3.3	omitted

Cultural characteristic #29 used.

Characteristic	A	B	C	D	E	F	Average	Item #
38. Feels that the extended family is important. (Extended family refers to "all recognized relatives on one's mother's and one's father's side, along with the kinsmen of one's spouse.) (Karner, 1969)	4	5	4 = 25/6	4	4	4	4.2	57
39. Believes in having many children. (Karner, 1969)	3	2	2 = 12/6	1	2	2	2	omitted

Revisions: This used to be true, but no longer is. (Dalven) (Toledano)

Characteristic	A	B	C	D	E	F	Average	Item #
40. Is not a strict observer with regard to use of kosher foods, religious and holiday ceremonies. (Gornick, 1975)	1	2	1 = 10/6	2	2	2	1.7	omitted

The following 21 cultural characteristics were added for weighting as a result of pilot respondent and expert suggestions, and after review and discussions with the panel of experts rating the original characteristics.

Characteristic	Expert						Average	Questionnaire Item #
	A	B	C	D	E	F		

Characteristic	A	B	C	D	E	F	Average	Questionnaire Item #
41. The idea of tradition is extremely important. (Expert addition)	5	5	5 = 27/6	3	5	4	4.5	52
42. Strict upbringing of children. (Pilot respondent addition)	4	3	4 = 23/6	3	5	4	3.8	65
43. Is a member of a close-knit community exemplified by informal clubs consisting of continuing group of same small community where backgrounds of most are similar. Is informally reserved for same group. Many are related to one another and know each other's background. Frequent socializing almost always within this close-knit community. (Pilot respondent addition)	2	4	3 = 21/6	3	4	5	3.5	61
44. Living up to the ways of elders is important. Consciousness of ways of elders.	4	5	2 = 18/6	1	3	3	3	58
45. Etiquette (social manners) emphasized in the society. (Expert addition)	4	5	1 = 18/6	4	2	2	3	50
46. In modern times, women with intellectual pursuits and job stamina would be more helped by men in the Sephardic community because they are also starved for the intellectual companionship, though they may not be aware of it. (Expert addition)	3	3	1 = 14/6	2	2	3	2.3	39

Omitted from analysis.

Characteristic	A	B	C	D	E	F	Average	Questionnaire Item #
47. Sephardim have a humanistic, intellectual, broad-minded approach to religion (as opposed to dogmatism, parochialism, and rigid denominationalism). (Expert addition)	5	5	3 = 24/6	5	4	2	4	44,45
48. If religious and orthodox, will not be too extreme, e.g., if a	1	1	2 = 17/6	5	4	4	2.8	28,36

Characteristic	Expert						Average	Questionnaire Item #
	A	B	C	D	E	F		

woman not too extreme lighting Kashrut, if a man in putting on Tefilim, or the family will not be too extreme eating only Kosher foods with separate set of dishes for meat and dairy, etc. (Pilot respondent addition)

Omitted from analysis.

49. Considers self worldly, sophis- 5 5 3 5 2 2
ticated and versatile by heri-   = 22/6   3.7   72
tage and personality. (Expert
addition)

50. Not aggressive group organizers 2 4 3 4 1 4
perhaps related to lack of   = 18/6   3   51
social aggressiveness. Refuses
to push too much for the sake of the Sephardic group. (Expert addition)

51. Sense of honor is extremely 5 5 4 4 5 5
important. The element of   = 28/6   4.7   40
honor and dignity looms largely
in the consciousness of Sephardim. (Expert addition)

52. Does not consider work with his 2 2 3 5 2 4
hands beneath his dignity. He   = 18/6   3   41
will not look on any kind of
work as being lowly. (Expert addition)

53. The Sephardic men and women 5 5 1 4 3 4
are innately creative and aes-   = 22/6   3.7   43
thetic. There is a strong aes-
theticism in the culture. (Expert addition)

54. Sephardim are fundamentalists 1 2 3 2 4 5
and stick to the basics: for   = 17/6   2.8   64
example, politically, family, etc.
would be conservative. (Pilot respondent addition)

55. Sephardim would give less 1 5 3 3 5 5
status to advanced academic   = 22/6   3.7   27

Characteristic	Expert						Average	Questionnaire Item #
	A	B	C	D	E	F		

titles than to financial success. (Expert addition)

56. If a man, and if engaged in a
dispute at business with a client
or customer, would give up his
point of view for the sake of good business. (Pilot respondent addition)

| | 1 | 4 | 1 | 4 | 3 | 1 | | |
| | | | $= 14/6$ | | | | 2.3 | 42 |

Omitted from analysis.

57. If the business was in trouble,
he would be very reluctant to
take a loan from a bank or
public place, but would turn to the family first. (Pilot respondent addition)

| | 2 | 5 | 1 | 1 | 3 | 1 | | |
| | | | $= 13/6$ | | | | 2.2 | 77 |

Omitted from analysis.

58. Men are good at business.
(Pilot respondent addition)

| | 3 | 3 | 1 | 2 | 4 | 5 | | |
| | | | $= 17/6$ | | | | 2.8 | 73 |

59. Strong emphasis on respect to
be shown to parents. (Expert
addition)

| | 5 | 5 | 3 | 5 | 5 | 4 | | |
| | | | $= 27/6$ | | | | 4.5 | 79 |

60. As a Sephardi, sense of seeing
self as belonging to an elite
group. Pride in Sephardic his-
tory of social and cultural prominence in old world countries of origin. (Pilot
respondent addition)

| | 4 | 5 | 4 | 4 | 4 | 4 | | |
| | | | $= 25/6$ | | | | 4.2 | 62 |

61. Girls should be raised more
strictly than boys. (Pilot
respondent addition)

| | 2 | 5 | 4 | 4 | 5 | 4 | | |
| | | | $= 24/6$ | | | | 4 | 48 |

Appendix B

Questionnaire as Presented to Participants

(slightly amended version for Early American group,
to include genealogical history in United States)

PLEASE READ THE QUESTIONS BELOW AND WRITE IN ANSWERS OR CHECK
AS INDICATED FOR EVERY QUESTION. THIS QUESTIONNAIRE HAS TWO
SECTIONS. THE FIRST ASKS FOR FACTUAL INFORMATION ABOUT YOUR
BACKGROUND. THE SECOND ASKS FOR YOUR THOUGHTS AND OPINIONS.
PLEASE ANSWER EVERY QUESTION.

SECTION I

1. Age: _____

2. Sex: [ ] Female   [ ] Male

3. a. What is your religious/ethnic affiliation?
    [ ] Sephardic
    [ ] Ashkenaze
    [ ] Christian
    [ ] Other: Specify _____

   b. If you follow the Sephardic tradition, which national group, or old world country
    of origin, do you most consider yourself a part of? (If you are a part of more
    than one group, for example your mother is from one country and your father from
    another, please indicate which group you feel closest to.)
    [ ] Bulgarian   [ ] Iranian
    [ ] Bukharian   [ ] Iraqian
    [ ] Egyptian   [ ] Moroccan
    [ ] English   [ ] Syrian
    [ ] Greek   [ ] Turkish
    [ ] Dutch   [ ] Other: (Specify): _____

4. a. Were you born in this country? [ ] Yes   [ ] No

   b. If no, when did you come to this country? _____

5. Which generation of your family is the first to come to this country?
    [ ] My own
    [ ] My parents
    [ ] My grandparents
    [ ] My great grandparents
    [ ] Other: (For example, father born in USA, mother born elsewhere)
    Specify: _____

6. My mother is (was):
    [ ] Sephardic
    [ ] Ashkenaze
    [ ] Christian
    [ ] Other: Specify _____

7. My father is (was):
    [ ] Sephardic
    [ ] Ashkenaze
    [ ] Christian
    [ ] Other: Specify _____

8. Birthplaces:
   City and Country: My own: _____
                        City   Country
                My mother: _____
                        City   Country
                My mother's mother: _____
                        City   Country
                My mother's father: _____
                        City   Country
                My father: _____
                        City   Country
                My father's mother: _____
                        City   Country
                My father's father: _____
                        City   Country

9. a. Are you presently employed?　　[ ] Yes　　[ ] No

   b. If yes, what is your occupation? _____

   c. If no, what is your status?
      [ ] Retired
      [ ] Student
      [ ] Housewife
      [ ] Other (Specify): _____

   d. If no, but have been previously employed, when is the last year you worked? _____

10. Your total income the last year you worked? (Not your spouse's):
    [ ] $ 0 - 9,999
    [ ] 10,000 - 19,999
    [ ] 20,000 - 29,999
    [ ] 30,000 - 49,999
    [ ] 50,000 - 74,999
    [ ] 75,000 or more
    [ ] I have never worked

11. Education (check highest level of education completed):
    [ ] Less than high school
    [ ] High school graduate
    [ ] Business school graduate
    [ ] College degree (two year)
    [ ] College degree (four year)
    [ ] Master's degree
    [ ] Other advanced degree (Specify): _____

12. Your marital status is:
    [ ] Single   [ ] Married   [ ] Widowed   [ ] Divorced

    IF YOU ARE SINGLE, PLEASE OMIT QUESTIONS 13, 14, and 15 AND GO DIRECTLY TO QUESTION 16

13. a. Your spouse is (was):
       [ ] Sephardic
       [ ] Ashkenaze
       [ ] Christian
       [ ] Other: Specify: _____

    b. Your spouse's birthplace: _____
                                         City   Country

    c. Your spouse's education (check highest level of education completed):
       [ ] Less than high school
       [ ] High school graduate
       [ ] Business school graduate
       [ ] College degree (two year)
       [ ] College degree (four year)
       [ ] Master's degree
       [ ] Other advanced degree (Specify): _____

14. a. Is your spouse presently employed?   [ ] Yes   [ ] No

    b. If yes, what occupation? _____

    c. If yes, or has been employed in the past, please give his or her total income
       (the last year he or she worked):
       [ ] $ 0 - 9,999
       [ ] 10,000 - 19,999
       [ ] 20,000 - 29,999
       [ ] 30,000 - 49,999
       [ ] 50,000 - 74,999
       [ ] 75,000 or more

15. a. Do you have children?   [ ] Yes   [ ] No

    b. If yes, how many? _____

16. a. Which language is usually spoken in your home? _____

b. Are other languages spoken in your home? [ ] Yes   [ ] No

c. If yes, which other languages are spoken? _____

_____

SECTION II

17. Which groups of Jews do you think of as Sephardic? _____

_____

18. How important are the following foods in your home life?

	Very Important	Important	Somewhat Important	Not very Important	Not at all Important
a. Lamb or veal cooked with vegetables or beans					
b. Rice, cous cous or cracked wheat (bulghur)					
c. Vegetables stuffed with rice or meat for example, squash or grape leaves (may be called yaprakas or yebra)					
d. Little folded pie crusts stuffed with meat, cheese or spinach (may be called borekas or sembousak)					
e. Okra (may be called bamias or bamya)					
f. Fruit, cheese, nuts or filla pastry for dessert					

19. How important to you is it that children be named after the parent's parents, even if living?
[ ] Very important
[ ] Important
[ ] Somewhat important
[ ] Not particularly important
[ ] Not at all important

20. How interested are you in your family's Sephardic roots and genealogy? (For example, do you speak with elders about it, read books about Sephardim, etc.)
[ ] Extremely interested
[ ] Very interested
[ ] Interested
[ ] Somewhat interested
[ ] Not interested

21. When you meet a Sephardic person, you ask about or are interested in his or her Sephardic roots and country of origin?
[ ] Every time
[ ] Very often
[ ] Often
[ ] Sometimes
[ ] Hardly ever

22. When you meet a Sephardic person, you want him or her to know that you are Sephardic:
[ ] Every time
[ ] Very often
[ ] Often
[ ] Sometimes
[ ] Hardly ever

23. When you meet an American Ashkenazi person, you want him or her to know that you are Sephardic?
 [ ] Every time
 [ ] Very often
 [ ] Often
 [ ] Sometimes
 [ ] Hardly ever

24. When you meet an American Gentile person, you want him or her to know that you are Sephardic:
 [ ] Every time
 [ ] Very often
 [ ] Often
 [ ] Sometimes
 [ ] Hardly ever

25. In your family, who makes the final decision, in actual practice, with regard to the following situations? If you are not married or parents are deceased, please answer on the basis of your ideal. (Please check one for each situation.)

	Husband	Wife	Joint Decision
a. Support of husband's parents			
b. Support of wife's parents			
c. Education of children			
d. Adequacy of income			
e. Vacations			
f. Socializing with others			

26. How often do you visit or are visited by other Sephardim as compared with your visiting of and by non-Sephardim?
 [ ] Much more with Sephardim than with non-Sephardim
 [ ] More with Sephardim than with non-Sephardim
 [ ] About the same with Sephardim as with non-Sephardim
 [ ] Less with Sephardim than with non-Sephardim
 [ ] Much less with Sephardim than with non-Sephardim

27. Do you give more respect to financial success or to advanced academic degrees?
 [ ] Much more respect to financial success
 [ ] More respect to financial success
 [ ] Financial success and advanced academic degrees are equal in importance
 [ ] More respect to advanced academic degrees
 [ ] Much more respect to advanced academic degrees

28. What best describes your practice of Judaism?
 [ ] Extremely religious
 [ ] Very religious
 [ ] Religious
 [ ] Somewhat religious
 [ ] Not religious

29. When you meet an American Ashkenazi person, you want him or her to know that you are Jewish:
 [ ] Every time
 [ ] Very often
 [ ] Often
 [ ] Sometimes
 [ ] Hardly ever

30. When you meet an American Gentile person, you want him or her to know that you are Jewish:
 [ ] Every time
 [ ] Very often
 [ ] Often
 [ ] Sometimes
 [ ] Hardly ever

93

31. Do you feel that you are different from people of the following groups?

	Yes, very different	Yes, different	Somewhat different	Not different	Undecided
a. Sephardim in general					
b. Sephardim of my own national group					
c. American Ashkenazim					
d. American Gentiles					
e. Israeli Jews					

32. Below is a list of communities. Indicate to what extent you feel close to each of these communities by checking one of the boxes for each community listed.

	Extremely close	Very close	Moderately close	Somewhat close	Not close
a. All Sephardim					
b. Sephardim of my own national group					
c. American Ashkenazim					
d. American Gentiles					
e. Sephardic Israelis					
f. All Israeli Jews					
g. Jews in Iran					

33. To what extent do you now feel pride as the relation of the following groups of people and events?

	Extremely proud of	Very proud of	Moderately proud of	Slightly proud of	Not proud of
a. Pioneer Pilgrims in Massachusetts					
b. Sephardic traditions and history					
c. Ashkenaze traditions and history					
d. Pioneer Israeli Jews					
e. Traditions and history of my own national group					

34. Do you feel that your hopes and aspirations are bound up with the hopes and aspirations of the following groups of people? Please check one box for each of the five groups.

	Yes, very strongly	Yes	Moderately	Slightly	No
a. All Sephardim					
b. Sephardim of my own national group					
c. American Ashkenazim					
d. American Gentiles					
e. Israeli Jews					

35. To what extent do you think what happens to the following groups of people in the future will influence the lives of your children?

	Very strong influence	Strong influence	Some influence	Slight influence	No influence
a. All Sephardim					
b. Sephardim of my own national group					
c. American Ashkenazim					
d. American Gentiles					
e. Israeli Jews					

36. How important is it to you to follow these religious customs? (Please check a box for each.)

	Extremely Important	Very Important	Important	Somewhat Important	Not Important
a. Keeping separate dishes for meat and dairy					
b. Lighting candles for the Sabbath					
c. Wearing a head covering or other religious identification in public					

PLEASE INDICATE IF YOU AGREE WITH THE FOLLOWING STATEMENTS

	Agree strongly	Agree	Undecided	Disagree	Disagree strongly
37. I have a great deal of pride in myself.					
38. I identify with Jews who suffered in the Holocaust.					
39. I would help a woman with intellectual pursuits and stamina.					
40. My sense of honor is of primary importance to me.					
41. Working with my hands is beneath my dignity.					
42. If there were an argument with a customer or client, one should give up one's point of view for the sake of good business.					
43. I am not a creative nor artistic person.					
44. Judaism should be seen as a strict and authoritarian consolidation of past learning.					
45. Judaism should be seen as a cherished antiquity and passed on to new generations, but an element of controversy in Judaism is appropriate.					
46. I feel very Sephardic					

	Agree strongly	Agree	Undecided	Disagree	Disagree strongly
47. I feel very Jewish.					
48. Girls should be raised more strictly than boys.					
49. I see present-day American Sephardim as a continuation of Sephardim throughout history all over the world.					
50. I am very aware of the social manners of myself and others.					
51. I work a lot to organize for the sake of the Sephardic group.					
52. The idea of tradition is important to me.					
53. The men should be felt by others to be the boss in the family.					
54. The place for women is in the home.					
55. It is important for Sephardim to marry Sephardim from their own national group.					
56. It is important for Sephardim to marry Sephardim no matter from which national group.					
57. My family is very important to me. (Family refers to relatives of your mother and father and those of your spouse's mother and father.)					
58. Living up to the ways of family elders is important to me.					
59. I do not attend large Sephardic gatherings.					
60. The hospitable entertaining of family, friends, or neighbors in my own home is important to me.					
61. I am a part of a Sephardic community where most of my socializing occurs. The community is close-knit and mostly reserved to people of similar backgrounds which are generally known.					
62. As a Sephardi, I feel connected to a group of people with a history of social and cultural prominence in their old world countries of origin.					
63. It is important to teach children Sephardic traditions and customs.					
64. With regard to politics and social issues, I am more likely to be conservative and traditional rather than liberal.					
65. Children should not be raised too strictly.					

	Agree strongly	Agree	Undecided	Disagree	Disagree strongly
66. Sephardic culture and history should not be explored because to do so divides us as Jews.					
67. Sephardic culture and history should be explored to promote a deeper understanding of our Jewish heritage.					
68. The idea of independence, especially financial independence, should be more emphasized for a boy than a girl. He should expect to be financially responsible for himself and/or a family.					
69. Most American Ashkenazim understand that Sephardim are socially diverse.					
70. Most American Gentiles understand that there are some differences between Ashkenaze and Sephardic culture.					
71. Most Sephardim consider me to be Sephardic.					
72. I am not a worldly wise person.					
73. I have a good business sense.					
74. Most American Ashkenazim understand the role of Sephardim in the development of America.					
75. Most Israeli Jews understand that Sephardim are socially diverse.					
76. Not every Jew should see himself as if he is a survivor of the Holocaust.					
77. If my family had financial trouble, I would turn first to a bank or other public place rather than family or friends.					
78. Most American Sephardim understand the role of Sephardim in the development of America.					
79. One must never show disrespect to one's parents.					
80. When I attend Synagogue, it is important that I attend one with a Sephardic service.					

THIS IS THE END OF THE QUESTIONNAIRE.
AGAIN, THANK YOU FOR YOUR TIME AND COOPERATION.

References

Adelson, J. (1950). A research in Jewish group identification. Unpublished doctoral dissertation, University of California.

Adelson, J. (1953). A study of minority group authoritarianism. In M. Sklare (Ed.) The Jews: Social patterns of an American group. New York: Free Press.

Adorno, T. W., Frenkel-Brunswik, E., Levinson, D. J., & Sanford, R. N. (1950). The authoritarian personality. New York: Harper.

Allport, G. W. (1958). The nature of prejudice. New York: Addison, Wesley, Inc.

Allport, G. W. (1966). Pattern and growth in personality. New York: Holt, Rinehart and Winston.

American Jewish Committee. (1978, March 13). The inclusion of a Sephardi dimension in American Jewish education. New Directions: A Publication of the Annual Workshop on Innovative Jewish Education.

Angel, M. D. (1971, March-April). Sephardic culture in America. Jewish Life, 38, 7-11.

Angel, M. D. (1971, June). "The grandees" a voice from Shearith Israel [Review of The Grandees]. Four reviews on Stephen Birmingham's book The Grandees. The Foundation for the Advancement of Sephardic Studies and Culture, Inc., Tract No. 9, 16-19.

Angel, M. D. (1973). The Sephardim of the United States: An exploratory study. The American Jewish Yearbook, 77-138.

Anisfeld, M., Monoz, S., & Lambert, W. E. (1966). The structure and dynamics of the ethnic attitudes of Jewish adolescents. Journal of Abnormal and Social Psychology, 66, 31-36.

Baltzell, E. D. (1966). The Protestant establishment: Aristocracy and caste in America. New York: Vintage Books.

Banks, G., Gerenson, B., Carkhoff, R. (1967). The Effects of counselor race and training upon the counseling process with Negro clients in initial interviews. Journal of Clinical Psychology, 23, 70-72.

Barron, M. L. (Ed.). (1962). American minorities: A textbook of readings in intergroup relations. New York: Alfred A. Knopf.

Benardete, M. J. (1953). Hispanic culture and character of the Sephardic Jews. New York: Hispanic Institute of the United States.

Birmingham, S. (1971). The Grandees. New York: Harper and Row.

Boas, F. (1911). The Mind of the primitive man. New York: Macmillan.

Bock, G. (1976). The Jewish schooling of American Jews: A study of non-cognitive educational effects. Unpublished doctoral dissertation, University of California.

Bogardus, E. S. (1967). A Forty year racial distance study. Los Angeles: University of Southern California.

Bonjean, C., Hill, R. J., & McLemore, S. D. (1967). Sociological measurement: An inventory of scales and indices. San Francisco: Chandler.

Brenner, L. O. (1960). Hostility and Jewish group identification. Unpublished doctoral dissertation, Boston University Graduate School.

Browne, R. S., & Rustin, B. (1968). Separatism or integration, which way for America? New York: National Jewish Community Relations Advisory Council.

Calia, V. F. (1966). The Culturally deprived client: A reformulation of the counselor's role. Journal of Counseling Psychology, 13, 100-105.

Campeas, H. J. (1971, June). The Inclusion of a Sephardi dimension in American Jewish education. New Directions: A Publication of the Annual Workshop on Innovative Jewish Education, 47-56.

Cardozo, D. A. (1965-66, Winter). Customs of the Sephardim. Jewish Heritage, 10, 10-14.

Carmichael, S., & Hamilton, C. V. (1967). Black Power: The politics of liberation in America. New York: Random House.

Cartwright, D. (Ed.). (1951). Field theory in social sciences. New York: Harper.

Cattell, R. B. (1966). The Handbook of multivariate experimental psychology. Chicago: Rand McNally.

Chammou, E. (1976). Migration and adjustment: The case of Sephardic Jews in Los Angeles. Unpublished doctoral dissertation, University of California at Los Angeles.

Chein, I., Deutsch, M., Hyman, H., & Jehoda, M. (Issue Eds.). (1949). Consistency and inconsistency in intergroup relations. Journal of Social Issues, V:3.

Chetnik, M., et al. (1967). A quest for identity: Treatment of disturbed Negro children in a predominantly white treatment center. American Journal of Orthopsychiatry, 71-77.

Clark, K., & Clark, M. (1950). Emotional factors in racial identification and preference in Negro children. Journal of Negro Education, 19, 341-350.

Cobbs, P. (1972). Ethnotherapy in groups. In New perspectives on encounter groups. San Francisco: Jossey-Bass, Inc., 383-403.

Cohen, Eli. (1977). On the nature of Jewish identity: A methodological approach. Unpublished doctoral dissertation, Indiana University.

Cohen, H. J. (1971). Sephardi Jews in the United States: Marriage with Ashkenazim and non-Jews. Dispersion and Unity, 151-160.

Cohen, S. (1974). The impact of Jewish education on religious identification and practice. Jewish Social Studies, 36, 316-326.

Cronbach, L. J. (1971). Test validation. In R. Thorndike (Ed.), Educational measurement. Washington, DC: American Council on Education.

Dalven, R. (Ed.). (1978). The Sephardic scholar (Series 3). New York: American Society of Sephardic Studies.

Dashefsky, A. (1975). Theoretical frameworks in the study of ethnic identity: Toward a social psychology of ethnicity. Ethnicity, 2, 10-18.

Dashefsky, A., & Shapiro, N. (1974). Ethnic identification among American Jews. Lexington, MA: Lexington Books.

Dobrinsky, Rabbi H. C. (1978, March 13). The Inclusion of a Sephardi dimension in American Jewish education. In Proceedings of the Annual Workshop on New Directions in Jewish Education. New York: The American Jewish Committee, Conference on Innovative Projects in Jewish Education.

Dollard, J. (1937). Caste and class in a southern town. New Haven: Yale University Press.

101

Driedger, L. (1976). Ethnic self-identity: A comparison of ingroup evaluations. Sociometry, 39(2), 131-141.

Durkheim, E. (1947). The Division of labor in society (G. Simpson, Trans.). Glencoe, IL: The Free Press. (Original work published 1893)

Erikson, E. H. (1968). Childhood and society (rev. ed.). New York: Norton.

Erikson, E. H. (1959). Identity and the life cycle: Selected papers. Psychological Issues, I.

Erikson, E. H. (1956). The Problem of ego identity. The Journal of American Psychoanalytic Association, 4, 56-121.

Etzioni-Halevy, E., & Shapira, R. (1975). Jewish identification of Israeli students: What lies ahead. Jewish Social Studies, 37, 251-266.

Farago, U. (1972). The influence of a Jewish summer camp's social climate on campers' Jewish identity. Unpublished doctoral dissertation, Brandeis University.

Faur, J. (1978, March 13). The Inclusion of a Sephardi dimension in American Jewish education. In Proceedings of the Annual Workshop on New Directions in Jewish Education. New York: The American Jewish Committee, Conference on Innovative Projects in Jewish Education.

Faur, J. (1972, Summer). Why Sephardim? The Sephardic World, I(1).

Foundation for the Advancement of Sephardic Studies and Culture. Tracts and publications.

Frazier, E. F. (1949). The Negro in the United States. New York: Macmillan Co.

Friedman, M. (Ed.). (1971). Overcoming middle class rage. Philadelphia: Westminster Press.

Gans, H. J. (1962). The Urban villagers. New York: The Free Press.

Gans, H. (1973). More equality. New York: Random House.

Geismar, L. A. (1954). A Scale for the measurement of ethnic identification. Jewish Social Studies, 16, 33-60.

Giordano, J. (1972). Ethnicity and mental health. New York: National Project on Ethnic America, American Jewish Committee.

Glazer, N., & Moynihan, D. P. (1970, 1963). Beyond the melting pot. Cambridge, MA: Harvard University Press and M. I. T. Press.

Glazer, N., & Moynihan, D. (1975). Ethnicity theory and experience. Cambridge: Harvard Press.

Glock, C., & Stark, R. (1965). Religion and society in tension. Chicago: Rand McNally.

Goldstein, S., & Goldscheider, C. (1968). Jewish Americans: Three generations in a Jewish community. Englewood Cliffs, NJ: Prentice-Hall.

Gordon, M. M. (1964). Assimilation in American life: The role of race, religion and national origins. New York: Oxford University Press.

Gornick, V. (1975, Summer). Sephardim of the east: The differences run deep. Present Tense, I(4), 44-49.

Gould, J., & Kolb, W. L. (Eds.). (1964). A Dictionary of the social sciences. Glencoe, IL: Free Press.

Greeley, A. M. (1977). The American Catholic. New York: Random House.

Greeley, A. M. (1971a). Why can't they be like us?: America's white ethnic groups. New York: E. P. Dutton & Co., Inc.

Greeley, A. M. (1971b). We and They: The differences linger. In M. Friedman (Ed.), Overcoming middle class rage. Philadelphia: Westminster Press.

Greeley, A. M. (1969). Why can't they be like us?: Facts and fallacies about ethnic differences and group conflicts in America. New York: Institute of Human Relations Press, The American Jewish Committee.

Gross, M. (1966). Exploration of the differences in preschool learning readiness and concomitant differences in certain cultural attitudes between two subcultural Jewish groups. Unpublished doctoral dissertation, Columbia University.

Hall, G. S., & Lindzey, G. (1957). Theories of personality. New York: John Wiley and Sons.

103

Hamburger, M. (1958). A Revised occupational scale for rating socioeconomic status. In Realism and consistency in early adolescent aspirations and expectations. Unpublished doctoral dissertation, Teacher's College, Columbia University.

Harris, T. K. (1979). The prognosis for Judeo-Spanish: Its description, present status, survival and decline with implications for language death in general. Unpublished doctoral dissertation, Georgetown University.

Hartley, E. (1946). Problems in prejudice. New York: King's Crown Press.

Hartley, E., Rosenbaum, M., & Schwartz, S. (1948). Children's perceptions of ethnic group membership. The Journal of Psychology, 26, 387-398.

Hendel-Sebestyen, G. (1969). The Sephardic home: Ethnic homogeneity and cultural traditions in a total institution. Unpublished doctoral dissertation, Columbia University.

Herman, S. N. (1977). Jewish identity: A social-psychological perspective. Beverly Hills, CA: Sage Publications.

Hewitt, M. L. (1980). But they're still Jews: Jewish identity, assimilation and the ethnogenesis model. Unpublished doctoral dissertation, University of Massachusetts.

Himmelfarb, H. (1977). The Interaction effects of parents, spouse and schooling: Comparing the impact of Jewish and Catholic schools. The Sociological Quarterly, 50, 114-129.

Himmelfarb, H. (1975). Measuring religious involvement. Social Forces, 53, 606-618.

Himmelfarb, H. (1980). The study of American Jewish identification: How it is defined, measured, obtained, sustained and lost. Journal for the Scientific Study of Religion, 19, 48-60.

Horowitz, R. (1939). Racial aspects of self-identification in nursery school children. The Journal of Psychology, 7, 91-99.

Hull, C. H., and Nie, N. H. (1981). SPSS update 7-9. New York: McGraw-Hill.

Isaacs, H. R. (1975). Idols of the tribe, group identity and political change. In N. Glazer and D. P. Moynihan (Eds.), Ethnicity Theory and Experience. New York: Harper and Row, 29-52.

Janov, A. (1960). A Study of differences in the priorities of Jewish identification. Unpublished doctoral dissertation, Claremont Graduate School, Claremont, CA.

Kallen, H. M. (1924). Culture and democracy in the United States. New York: Boni and Liveright.

Karner, F. P. (1969). The Sephardics of Curaçao: A study of sociocultural patterns in flux. Assen, The Netherlands: Van Gorcum and Comp, N.V.

Kelman, H. C. (1977). Foreword. In S. N. Herman, Jewish identity: A social-psychological perspective. Beverly Hills, CA: Sage Publications, 9-12.

Kerlinger, F. N. (1973). Foundations of behavioral research (2nd ed.). New York: Holt, Rinehart, Winston.

Klein, J. W. (1980). Jewish identity and self-esteem: Healing wounds through ethnotherapy. Institute on Pluralism and Group Identity of the American Jewish Committee.

Klineberg, O. (1967). The Multi-national society: Some research problems. Social Sciences Information, 6, 81-99.

Klineberg, O. (1935). Negro intelligence and selective migration. New York: Macmillan.

Krech, D., Crutchfield, R. S., Ballachey, E. L. (1962). Individual in society. New York: McGraw Hill.

Lazerwitz, B. (1978). An Approach to the components and consequences of Jewish identification. Contemporary Jewry, 4, 3-8.

Lazerwitz, B. (1977). The Community variable in Jewish identification. Journal for the Scientific Study of Religion, 16, 361-369.

Lazerwitz, B. (1973). Religious identification and its ethnic correlates: A multivariate model. Social Forces, 52, 204-220.

Lazerwitz, B. (1953, January). Some factors in Jewish identification. Jewish Social Studies, XV(1), 3-24.

Lenski, G. (1961). The Religion factor. New York: Doubleday.

Levita, D. J. (1965). The Concept of identity. New York: Basic Books.

105

Lewin, K. (1948). Resolving social conflicts. New York: Harper and Brothers.

Linesmith, A. R., and Strauss, A. L. (1958). Social psychology. New York: Rinehart and Winston.

Lipnick, B. (1976). An experiment that works in religious education. New York: Bloch.

Lipset, S. (1972). Group life in America: A task force report. New York: The American Jewish Committee, Institute of Human Relations.

Mac Corquodale, K., & Meehl, P. (1954). Operational validity of constructs. In M. Marx (Ed.), Psychological theory. New York: Macmillan Co.

MacIver, R. M., & Page, C. H. (1953). Society. London: Macmillan and Co.

Makabe, T. (1979). Ethnic identity scale and social mobility: The case of Nisei in Toronto. Canadian Review of Sociology and Anthropology, 16(2), 136-146.

Masuda, M., Matsumato, G., Meredith, G. (1970). Ethnic identity in three generations of Japanese Americans. The Journal of Social Psychology, 81, 199-207.

Mazur, A. C. (1969). Revitalized ethnicity: A study of Jewish social scientists. Unpublished doctoral dissertation, The Johns Hopkins University.

Mead, G. H. (1934). Mind, self and society. Chicago: University of Chicago Press.

Merrifield, P. (1984). Guidebook to multivariate techniques applied to psychoeducational problems. New York: Laboratory for Behavioral Measurement, Department of Educational Psychology, SEHNAP, New York University.

Miller, D. R. (1963). The study of social relationships: Structure, identity, and social interaction. In S. Koch (Ed.), Psychology: A Study (Vol. 5). New York: McGraw Hill, 1963.

The Minority within a minority. (1976, June). Human Behavior Magazine.

Mizrahi, J. (1987). Sources of diversity in Sephardim. UMI 8720134. Doctoral dissertation, New York University.

Mostwin, D. 91971). The Transplanted family--A study of social adjustment of the Polish immigrant family to the U.S. after the second world war. Unpublished doctoral dissertation, Columbia University, School of Social Work.

Newcomb, T. M. (1950). Social psychology. New York: The Dryden Press.

Nie, N. H., Hull, C. H., Jenkins, J. G., Steinbrenner, K. and Bent, D. H. (1975). SPSS. Statistical package for the social sciences (2nd ed.).

Papo. J. (1987). Sephardim in twentieth century America: In search of unity. San Jose, CA: Pele' Yoetz Books.

Papo, J. (1946). The Sephardic community of America. Reconstructionist, 12, 12-18.

Parsons, T. (1975). Some theoretical considerations on the nature and trends of change of ethnicity. In N. Glazer & D. P. Moynihan (Eds.), Ethnicity theory and experience. Cambridge: Harvard University Press, 53-83.

Patai, R. (1953). Israel between east and west. Philadelphia: Jewish Publication Society.

Patterson, C. H. (1959). Counseling and psychotherapy: Theory and practice. New York: Harper & Row.

Patterson, O. (1975). Context and choice in ethnic allegiance: A theoretical framework and Caribbean case study. In N. Glazer & D. P. Moynihan (Eds.), Ethnicity theory and experience. Cambridge: Harvard University Press, 308-309.

Pederson, P. B. (1978, April). Four dimensions of cross-cultural skill in counselor training. Personnel and Guidance Journal, 56(8), 480-484.

Petegorsky, D. S. (1941, September). The Strategy of hatred. Antioch Review, I, 377.

Pitchon, M. (1975, April 18). Is Sephardism alive? Jewish Chronicle, 11.

Pollack, G. (1961). Graduates of Jewish day schools: A follow-up study. Unpublished doctoral dissertation, Western Reserve University.

Pressey, S. L., and Pressey, L. C. (1933). A comparison of the emotional development of Indians belonging to different tribes. Journal of Applied Psychology, XVII, 535-541.

Proshansky, H., & Newton, P. (1968). The Nature and meaning of Negro self-identity. In Deutsch, Katz, & Jensen (Eds.), Social class, race and psychological development. New York: Holt Rinehart & Winston, 178-219.

Random House Dictionary. (1966).

Riessman, F. (1969). Strategies and suggestions for training non-professionals. In B. Guerney (Ed.), Psychotherapeutic agents: New roles for nonprofessionals, parents and teachers. New York: Holt, Rinehart and Winston.

Rinder, I. D. (1959). Polarities in Jewish identification: The personality of ideological extremities. In R. Sklare (Ed.), The Jews: Social patterns of an American group. New York: Free Press, 493-502.

Rose, A. M. (1962). A Systematic summary of symbolic interaction theory. In Rose (Ed.), Human behavior and social processes. Boston: Houghton Miflin, 3-19.

Rose, A. M., & Rose, C. B. (1965). Group identification and the minority community. In A. M. Rose & C. B. Rose (Eds.), Minority problems. New York: Harper and Row, 247-252.

Rosen, B. (1976). Adolescence and religion. Cambridge, MA: Schenkman.

Roucek, J., & Brown, F. (1937). Our racial and national minorities. New York: Prentice Hall.

Rutchik, A. (1968). Self-esteem and Jewish identification. Jewish Education, 38(2), 40-46.

Sandberg, N. (1974). Ethnic identity and assimilation: The Polish-American community. New York: Praeger Publishers.

Sanua, V. D. (1967, June). A Study of the adjustment of Sephardi Jews in the New York metropolitan area. Jewish Journal of Sociology, IX(1), 25-33.

Schermerhorn, R. A. (1969). Comparative ethnic relations: A framework for theory and research. New York: Random House.

Segalman, R. (1967). Jewish identity scales: A report. Jewish Social Studies, 29, 92-111.

Segalman, R. (1966). My self hatred among Jews: A test of the Lewinian hypothesis of marginality of Jewish leadership. Unpublished doctoral dissertation, New York University.

The Sephardi world. (1979, April). Finding answers to Jewish education. New York: American Sephardi Federation, 6-7.

The Sephardic World. (1972). New York: World Institute for Sephardic Studies, I-II.

Sherif, M., & Sherif, C. W. (1953). Groups in harmony and tension. New York: Harper and Brothers.

Sherif, M., & Sherif, C. W. (1969). Social psychology. New York: Harper and Row.

Shibutani, T., & Kwan, K. (1965). Ethnic stratification. New York: Macmillan Co.

Sklare, M., & Greenblum, J. (1967). Jewish identity on the suburban frontier. New York: Basic Books.

Slotkin, J. S. (1955). Culture and psychopathology. Journal of Abnormal Social Psychology, 51, 269-275.

Steiner, S. (1968). The New Indians. New York: Dell Publishing Co.

Stern, S. (1977). The Sephardic Jewish community of Los Angeles: A study in folklore and ethnic identity. Unpublished doctoral dissertation, Indiana University.

Strauss, A. L. (1959). Mirrors and masks: The search for identity. Glencoe: The Free Press.

Sullivan, H. S. (1953). The Interpersonal theory of psychiatry. New York: Norton.

Sutton, J. (1979). Magic carpet: Aleppo-in-Flatbush. New York: Thayer-Jacoby.

Tamir, V. (1979, March 11). Paper presented at eleventh annual Sephardic cultural festival of the American Society of Sephardic Studies, a talk marking the appearance of her book, Bulgaria and her Jews, published by Yeshiva University Press and Sepher-Hermon Press, Inc. At Yeshiva University.

Thomas, W. I., and Znaniecki, F. (1958). The Polish peasant in America. New York: Dover Publications.

Tonu, P. (1976). The nature of ethnic identity. Unpublished doctoral dissertation, Yale University.

Vail, S. (1970). The Effects of socio-economic class, race and level of experience in social workers' judgement of clients. Smith College Studies in Social Work, 40(3).

Verbit, M. (1970). The components and dimensions of religious behavior: Toward a reconceptualization of religiosity. In P. E. Hammond & B. Johnson (Eds.), American mosaic: Social patterns of religion in the U.S. New York: Random House.

Warner, W. L. (1953). American life. Chicago: University of Chicago Press.

Weber, M. (1961). The Ethnic group. In T.Parsons, et al. (Eds.), Theories of society. Glencoe, IL: Free Press, Vol. I, 305-309.

Weiss, S. (1957). Acceptance of Jews and Gentiles by Jewish children. Unpublished doctoral dissertation, New York University.

Wheelis, A. (1958). The quest for identity. New York: Norton.

Wirth, L. (1964). On cities and social life. Chicago: University of Chicago Press.

Wolfson, R. (1974). A Description and analysis of an innovative living experience in Israel--The dream and the reality. Unpublished doctoral dissertation, Washington University.

Yerkes, R. M. (Ed.). (1921). Psychological examining in the U.S. Army. Memoirs of the National Academy of Science, XV.

Youcha, G. (1973, Summer). The not so grandees. The National Jewish Monthly, 88, 68-75.

Zak, I. (1972). Jewish background, self-esteem, Jewish-American identity, and attitudes toward Israel. Unpublished doctoral dissertation, New York University.

Zangwill, I. (1909). The Melting pot. New York: The Macmillan Co.

Zenner, W. P. (1968, June). Syrian Jews in three social settings. The Jewish Journal of Sociology, X, 101-121.

Zion, Sidney. (1971, April 18). [Review of The Grandees]. The New York Times Book Review, 5.